Marriage 911: First Response

Hope for Your Marriage

Harmony for Your Home

NATIONAL INSTITUTE OF MARRIAGE

IN PARTNERSHIP WITH

JOE AND MICHELLE WILLIAMS

WORKBOOK

MARRIAGE 911: FIRST RESPONSE

> *Hope for Your Marriage*
> *Harmony for Your Home*

National Institute of Marriage

In Partnership with Joe and Michelle Williams

ALL RIGHTS RESERVED

For information on the Marriage 911 program, call the National Institute of Marriage, at (417) 335-5882. Or e-mail us at: nationalmarriage.com. Our mailing address is: 2175 Sunset Inn Road, Branson, MO 65616.

No part of this material may be reproduced or photocopied, except as provided by USA copyright law.

All Scripture quotations are taken from HOLY BIBLE, NEW INTERNATIONAL VERSION. Copyright 1973, 1978, 1984 by International Bible Society. Used by permission of Zondervan Publishing House. All rights reserved.

The "NIV" and "New International Version" trademarks are registered in the United States Patent and Trademark Office by International Bible Society. Use of either trademark requires the permission of International Bible Society.

Originally written in 1997 as *Reconciling God's Way*, by Joe and Michelle Williams. Revised and renamed *Marriage 911: First Response* in 2007 by National Institute of Marriage and the International Center for Reconciling God's Way.

Use of *Marriage 911: First Response* name and logo with permission only.

Copyright © 2015 Joe and Michelle Williams
All rights reserved.
ISBN: 978-1-941733-32-5

Published by EA Books Publishing,
a division of Living Parables of Central Florida, Inc. a 501c3
eabooksonline.com

WELCOME FROM NATIONAL INSTITUTE OF MARRIAGE
www.nationalmarriage.com

As you prepare to begin your journey through this workbook, we want you to know our hearts and prayers are with you. We know your marriage is in some degree of distress, perhaps severe crisis, and we have dedicated our lives to help in situations just like yours. At NIM you'll find our team has a wide variety of training and experience but are all dedicated to one single passion: great relationships. For us, few things in life are more important than helping people experience the kind of fulfilling, meaningful relationships that the Lord desires for them to have. We believe every marriage is worth saving, and every couple can experience the promise of a great marriage. In fact, we believe that the relationships of those who follow Christ should be so extraordinary, that those around them are inspired to develop great relationships with God, self, and others as well.

All of that may sound impossible to you right now, and perhaps you feel as if you need a miracle! At our offices in Branson, Missouri and Rome, Georgia we run the equivalent of a Marriage Emergency Room. We have worked with thousands of couples that everybody had given up on including the couples themselves. The only requirement we have in order to work with them is a "yes" answer to this question:"If God were to work a miracle in your marriage, and the miracle could be the magnitude of the parting of the Red Sea, would you accept it?" That's it. All they have to do is be willing to receive what God may provide for them, even if they may think it impossible. Oh, and by the way, we define a miracle as a marriage with which both people are thrilled ...nothing more, nothing less!

The exciting news is that we witness God doing those types of miracles every single week. Our Lord is alive and well, is passionate about great relationships, and will not withhold Himself from an open and willing heart.

It is our joy and privilege, in partnership with Joe and Michelle Williams, to present this powerful program to you today. Originally written by the Williams in 1997, these books are a newly revised and updated collaboration between our two ministries. We have enthusiastically joined forces, working together more effectively than either ministry could alone. Therefore, the word "we" will refer to statements from all of us, unless otherwise noted.

This program may be all that is needed to open the door for your friend in crisis to experience a life-changing miracle personally and relationally, or it may be just the beginning. Either way, we appreciate your willingness to partner with us and the Williams, and be used as one of God's instruments on this journey. You may even get to witness a miracle! Our entire team at this very moment is standing with you in spirit and in prayer. May God richly bless you for your faithfulness, care, and sacrifice.

Dr. Robert S. Paul and Mark Pyatt
Co-Presidents, National Institute of Marriage

FOREWORD

The book you have in your hands could trigger a radical change in your life, or the life of someone you care about! I have a host of marriage related books on my office shelf, along with audio and video tapes, but for the specific task of initiating reconciliation in broken relationships even the most disastrous relationships — I look to this workbook as the best practical resource in conjunction with the Bible!

What makes this book so effective? It focuses on God and His plan for marriage and the dynamics of Christ centered relationships. It drives us right back to Scripture. In fact, before you go any further, stop reading and place your Bible right next to this book. You must read this book in tandem with God's Word. This book will not solve your marriage problems, reconcile your relationships with family members or friends, or bring your stubborn spouse back into your home. God does all that. This book will show you how to get out of God's way and allow Him to do the healing!

You are about to be blessed by the life experience of the authors, Joe and Michelle Williams. They are God focused, and have personally felt the brokenness of rebellious hearts and demolished marriages. They have "been there, done that." On the other hand, they have also experienced the awesome power of God's healing in their lives after submitting themselves totally to Him! They have climbed the high mountain, endured tremendous pain, and fallen on their knees before God bringing personal sacrifices of "a broken spirit; a broken and contrite heart..." (Psalm 51:17). The Lord responded by bathing them in grace and love, and healing their relationship. Having given them that gift, He also asked them to disciple others who have gone through or are going through the same heart rending challenges. They have had a solid, Christ centered marriage, and have our full support as the Directors of the Reconciling God's Way Ministry here in Modesto. This workbook is not an exercise in theory, it is born of life experience and Divine healing. This workbook is a sacrifice to God in grateful appreciation of His love and the ministry of reconciliation. As Joe and Michelle candidly share their experiences in this book, you will begin to see how God's promises affect our lives in powerful, eternal ways. Get ready to be blessed! And remember to give God the glory as you see Him work in your life, and in the lives of others.

Michael D. Douglass
Founder and Director of
Advancing Vibrant Communities Modesto, California

Contents

I. WHERE'S YOUR FOCUS?

pg. 2   1. Unmet Needs: Do You Expect Your Spouse To Meet All Your Needs?

pg. 6   2. Selfless Behavior: Are You Playing God By Trying to Meet All Your Spouse's Needs?

pg. 10   3. Caring for Self: Are You Exhausted and Feeling Hopeless?

pg. 15   4. Valuing Differences: Do You Want the Freedom to Be Who You Are?

II. WHERE'S YOUR HEART?

pg. 27   5. Secret Motives: Do You Really Want to Reconcile?

pg. 33   6. Secret Anger: Understand Your Anger...Revolutionize Your Marriage!

pg. 40   7. Secret Lies: Honesty Is At The Core Of True Intimacy

pg. 45   8. Secret Fears: What Keeps You From Being Real With Your Mate?

III. WHERE'S YOUR HOPE?

pg. 55   9. Know How To Recognize Hope: Bad Habits Are Hard To Break

pg. 63   10. Know What To Avoid: God's Timing Is Not Always Ours

pg. 71   11. Know Who's On Your Team: Turn Opposition Into Optimism

pg. 80   12. Know When To "Go Forth": Whatever The Outcome, Use It For Good

INTRODUCTION

When we separated as Christians in 1986, we were angry, confused, and wondered where the church was in our seemingly hopeless situation. We wanted desperately to be a happy Christian couple with a godly marriage. Nothing we tried seemed to work. In looking back, we now see that God, in His infinite wisdom and timing, had a plan and because we kept focused on Him during our separation, He allowed us to be a part of that plan.

We were separated for two years, and while it was lonely, painful, and embarrassing, we know now that God was grooming us for the ministry of reconciliation—His way. One of the things we lacked during our separation was a Christian couple who could come alongside us to love us, hold us accountable, and give us some tools for reconciling our marriage. The married couples we knew in the church either tried to rescue and fix our marriage (thus "burning out" in their frustrations) or avoided us altogether because of the lack of knowing what to say or do for us (we mistook this for not caring).

Because we had both experienced divorces in our past, we were determined to find how to deal with our marriage problems and avoid another failure. We knew that God hated divorce (Malachi 2:16), and we wanted to keep the marriage vows that we made as Christians. Through trial and error, and our sincere desire to obey God, we were able to reconcile.

We have been serving in the ministry of reconciliation since 1990, and are now Directors of Reconciling God's Way—a ministry dealing with marriages in crisis. It is our prayer that this workbook will allow you to have what we didn't. If your marriage is in a crisis, and your situation looks hopeless, here is an opportunity to reconcile—God's way!

Joe Williams
Michelle Williams
Modesto, California

BEFORE YOU BEGIN

Materials needed: Bible, journal or notebook, and your own copy of the workbook. It is also highly recommended that you read Yes, Your Marriage Can Be Saved, by Joe and Michelle Williams. This book will be a great supplement to the workbook, and will help you apply the concepts to your life in a more practical way.

You will need a couple of days to establish your support system as you prepare to go through the workbook. How you use the tools in the workbook, and how long it takes before you begin to experience major changes in your marriage, will depend on the following circumstances:

- *Whether or not your spouse is willing to participate.*
- *Whether you are separated or living together.*
- *Whether a third party, substance abuse, or physical abuse is involved.*
- *Your (and your spouse's) relationship with God.*
- *Your ability to meet regularly with your support person.*
- *Your sincere desire to reconcile.*
- *Your sincere desire to obey God.*

The tools in this workbook can be used in whatever circumstance you are facing. In the rare case where both you and your spouse want to reconcile at the same time, and both have a desire to obey God, the reconciliation process could take place very quickly. In those cases, we have witnessed marriages completely transformed within three months!

Chances are, however, that you are beginning this workbook with one of you more willing than the other. Some of you have a spouse who has no desire to even look at the workbook, and others of you may experience a willing spouse who becomes unwilling. Don't get discouraged. Joe and Michelle were off and on so often during their separation that it's a wonder they reconciled at all. Just remember that God is the God of miracles. While it's true that it takes two to reconcile a relationship, it only takes one of you to make the commitment to begin the process. **Let your spouse know that you are going through the material and give him/her information on how to purchase the workbook. Then don't mention it again, and pray! Let God do the rest. A lot can happen in three months, and this is your opportunity to do things God's way!**

CREATE YOUR SUPPORT SYSTEM

The most important thing you will do, after making the commitment to reconcile, is to put together your support system. Without prayer and accountability you will not be strong enough to stand against the opposition of the enemy and bring harmony to your home. It will take supernatural power from God and the support of Christian friends.

First, ask a Christian person (of your same gender) with a strong commitment to God and marriage if they would be willing to be your support person as you go through the workbook. This would require meeting with them twelve times for one hour per week, in order to go over the discussion questions at the end of each chapter. We have found it to work best when the meetings are weekly to help you stay consistent and accountable. If you and your spouse are working through this program, your support partners should not be a married to each other. The reasons for this guideline is explained in the Marriage 911: First Response Support Partner Handbook. Your support person will need a copy of the Support Partner Handbook, which is available through our ministry if you did not receive one with this workbook.

Next, prayerfully choose two or three Christian friends of your same gender who are supportive of your decision to have a good marriage and who will also help keep you accountable. Friendships that will encourage you to honor your spouse in words and actions during this time, and who will pray for your marriage, will be very important. It may also mean that you will have to distance yourself from people who encourage the opposite. If you are separated, avoid singles groups and any social setting that could cause you to become "friends" with someone of the opposite sex. Separations that end in divorce often have a third party involved. List the names and numbers of supportive friends who come to mind:

BE PREPARED

You're about to begin a process that the enemy does not want to happen. As long as Satan can divide families and keep homes broken, he has a better chance of destroying children and stopping the gospel of Christ from being spread. You are stepping into a battlefield, so be prepared. Read Ephesians 6:10-17, and plan on arranging your schedule to include the time that you'll need for prayer and workbook exercises.

We believe strongly in the power of prayer, and even though we may never personally meet you, we feel a connection with you because you are using our material. We realize that you are quite possibly going through some of the same things many of us have gone through in our own marriages. We would like to ask you to visit the back of your resource at this time and fill out a brief prayer form and send it to our team at NIM. We will keep your information confidential, and only a small prayer team will read what you write for the purpose of lifting you up to the Lord and possibly mailing you a card.

WHERE'S YOUR FOCUS?
Your marriage crisis is more about you and God than it is about you and your spouse.

"Set your minds on things above, not on earthly things" (Colossians 3:2).

WEEK ONE

Unmet Needs

Do you expect your spouse to meet all your needs?

From Joe: *I thought when I met Michelle that she was the perfect one for me. I didn't take into consideration what she was bringing in from her past, and I thought that her desire to meet all my needs meant that she loved me. I had unrealistic expectations of her, and when she let me down I felt unloved and rejected by her.*

If you identify with Joe's statement and feel that your spouse has let you down because of unmet needs in your life, maybe it's because of unrealistic expectations. It is impossible to expect another human being to be perfect enough to meet all your needs, but it is reasonable to want your needs to be satisfied. Between you and God, there are hosts of righteous and empowering ways for this to be accomplished.

Reconciliation Tool — 1A
"The Three-Month Crisis Plan"

There are 31 chapters of proverbs in the Bible (see Proverbs). For the next three months read a chapter in Proverbs each day while doing the workbook. In a journal or notebook, write down daily what God shows you in His Book of Wisdom. By communicating with God through His written word, your relationship with Him will grow, and your focus will begin to shift to Him to meet the needs that your mate cannot or will not meet. This "three-month crisis plan" is important because if your understanding of God's Word is limited, and you don't know how to recognize His instructions for our lives, it will be impossible to reconcile His way! Try to continue reading a chapter of Proverbs a day even after the three-months is over.

Reconciliation Tool 1B
"The Self-Nurture List"

Make a list of 10-20 activities that you enjoy doing alone that are not immoral, illegal, or expensive. Begin now to implement at least half of the activities you listed into your life each week. One thing we notice in people whose marriages are in crisis (and it was certainly true for the Williams), is that they seem to have lost a sense of themselves as individuals. The stresses of marriage troubles and everyday demands have replaced the simple enjoyments in life. If you have never spent time without your spouse just enjoying life's little pleasures, or if you thought marriage meant that you no longer should or could spend any time on your own, you have been missing out on the ability to nurture yourself and become a more fulfilled person. You shouldn't use the excuse that there's not enough time or that everyone else needs you. Remember, if you aren't taking responsibility to meet some of your own needs, you won't have sufficient energy, peace, and joy in your life you need as you try to meet the needs of others. You can't give what you don't have, and if you make your well-being primarily

WHERE IS YOUR FOCUS?: WEEK ONE — UNMET NEEDS

dependent on others you become powerless; you're well if they do what you want, you're not well if they don't.

List of Activities

(Examples: walking, biking, attending a movie or sports activity, window shopping, going for ice-cream or coffee, reading, listening to music.)

1.

2.

3.

4.

5.

6.

7.

8.

9.

10.

11.

12.

13.

14.

15.

WEEK ONE DISCUSSION QUESTIONS

Read the following questions and write in your answers in order to discuss them with your support partner during your weekly meeting time:

 Open in prayer

1. What are your hopes for going through the Marriage 911: First Response program?

2. How did you and your spouse meet? When you were dating your spouse what were the qualities that made you enjoy his/her company?

3. What expectations did you have about your spouse before you got married?

4. Did any of those qualities lead you to believe that he/she was going to be the man/woman of your dreams?

5. Explain your current relationship to God in comparison to how it's been in the past.

6. What was one thing that God showed you in your study of Proverbs this week?

7. What "self-nurture activities" did you do this week? If none, what is your reason?

8. Share any additional thoughts, insights from the Lord, or experiences that have happened this week that challenged your thinking or impacted your heart.

9. What is one specific concern for which you would like prayer this week?

 Close in prayer

NOTES

WEEK TWO

Selfless Behavior

Are you trying to play God by trying to meet all your spouse's needs?

From Michelle: *When I met Joe I was just getting over the pain of a divorce. I desperately wanted to give my love and affection to someone and to feel needed. I felt loved by Joe, and I enjoyed that I was able to make him happy. After we married, and reality set in, I felt smothered and controlled by his unrealistic expectations for me to meet all his needs.*

Many people believe their ability to make someone happy makes them more loveable or more valuable, and as a result will lead to them being loved. Being needed can certainly be affirming. In the beginning of this type of a relationship both parties are usually thrilled with this set-up. But if the happiness of one's spouse becomes the focus of life as an attempt to secure love, it can be just as self- centered as the person who expects their spouse to meet all of his/her needs. In either case, the focus is off God, and He considers this idolatry (see Exodus 20: 1-6). Sadly, this misguided focus not only distracts you and your spouse from God, but it also leads to feelings of resentment. At some point it becomes clear that no matter what you do, it will never be enough to secure happiness. Trying to be your spouse's "everything" is impossible and gives way to resignation. At the very same time, your spouse will resent feeling controlled and disappointed. What one can meaningfully offer a relationship - mutual support, caring and encouragement - is never fully realized.

Reconciliation Tool 2A
"Encourage Your Spouse"

1. **If your spouse is going through the workbook with you, join him/her in doing the self-nurture activity list.** Sit down together when your lists are completed, and encourage each other to take time in your lives to implement the activities. Help one another to make room in busy schedules (i.e., share child care responsibilities, transportation, and daily chores).

2. **Write a note to encourage your spouse to begin any activity he/she once enjoyed but has given up.** You may have to go back to when you met, remembering hobbies and interests your spouse had that did not include you. Remember, the activities must not be immoral, illegal, or expensive. Sincerely ask God to reveal any role you may have played in your spouse giving up this activity. As you gain clarity, apologize and ask for their forgiveness.

You may find writing a note a bit stretching, especially if you feel that your spouse is self-centered and demanding, or if you are unsure of your spouse's response to the note. If you feel that you can verbally communicate to your spouse easier, then do that, but don't neglect this exercise; we have found that with this tool most couples have been able to begin the process of rebuilding mutual respect for one another and let go of some resentment. Later, as the tension eases between the two of you, and you both are willing, you can combine your lists and choose activities that the two of you can do together as well. Some of the best conversations a couple can have often take place when you are sharing activities together.

WHERE IS YOUR FOCUS?: WEEK TWO — SELFLESS BEHAVIOR

From Michelle: *Change in behavior (even good change, like taking pressure off one another to meet every need) will sometimes create insecurities which can result in negative feelings and behavior. Prior to our separation, anytime one of us wanted to participate in an activity that didn't include the other it was seen as a threat. When we reconciled, we both realized that all the little interests we had added in our lives actually made us more attractive to the other, and we became more fulfilled individuals. Now, if one of us wants to take a class, go off in the other room for a quiet time of reading or listening to music, or engage in one of the activities on our list, we encourage one another instead of resist individual growth.*

From Joe: *I realize now that all those times that Michelle wanted time alone to think, write, read, or go off somewhere to "spend some time with God", were not because she didn't enjoy my company. I guess I realized it when I put it in the context of my liking to wash and wax my car alone. We enjoy different activities apart from one another, and I see now how important it is for us to be individuals. We are much happier now when we do spend time together.*

WEEK TWO DISCUSSION QUESTIONS

Read the following questions and write in your answers in order to discuss them with your support partner during your weekly meeting time:

 Open in prayer

1. Which has been more of a struggle for you: trying to be "the" source of your spouse's happiness or making your spouse "the" source of your happiness? Please explain.

2. In looking at it now, how productive has your approach been? How has it left you feeling about your spouse and your marriage? How has your approach left you feeling about you?

3. Did you write your spouse a note of encouragement? If not, why? If so, what response, if any, did you receive?

4. Did God reveal to you any part you may have played in your spouse giving up an enjoyed activity? Please describe.

5. What was one thing that God showed you in your study of Proverbs this week?

6. What "nurture activities" did you do this week? Did you and your spouse discuss any activities that you could begin doing again?

7. How well have you done in establishing a support network? Explain.

8. Share any additional thoughts, insights from the Lord, or experiences that have happened this week that challenged your thinking or impacted your heart.

9. Share one thing for which you are thankful and one concern.

 Close in prayer.

NOTES

WEEK THREE

Caring for Self
Are you exhausted and feeling hopeless?

From Joe: *When Michelle and I started having problems in our marriage, I tried everything I knew to keep our relationship from ending in separation and divorce. But each time we argued, I became so frustrated that I actually ended up saying and doing the exact opposite of what I knew I should.*

From Michelle: *All I wanted was peace in our home, but it seemed the harder I tried, the worse things got. I mistook Joe's frustration as not caring, and I finally just quit trying. Things looked hopeless to me by the time we separated, and I actually felt relief because I was so tired of trying to keep peace.*

In looking back, Joe and Michelle were able to see how having their focus on each other and trying to hold their shaky marriage together was wearing them both out. If their focus had been on God, and if they had been able to make wise decisions in the midst of their disagreements, neither of them would have been so exhausted. They started attending church in hopes that it would strengthen their marriage, but it wasn't until a few years later that they understood what it was to live a life of obedience to the Lord Jesus Christ. That understanding only took place as they spent time in God's Word, attended church and Bible study regularly, and spent time alone in prayer.

If you are not a member of a Bible-teaching church and attending a Bible study regularly, it will be difficult for you to know how God is directing you in daily decisions. Choosing to do things God's way in the midst of stressful circumstances takes supernatural strength and power that can only come from the Holy Spirit and a clear understanding of Scripture.

Reconciliation Tool 3A
"Spend a Day with God"

You have been spending time in Proverbs the past couple of weeks. Hopefully you have been able to write in your journal (or in the margins of your Bible for those of you who have a hard time journaling), about what God is revealing to you in His Book of Wisdom. Just as spending time in His Word is important, so is spending time alone with Him in prayer. Jesus spent many hours alone with God, and He showed us by example how to communicate with Him in prayer. Having a great relationship with God is the only thing that can change your relationship with one another.

The only way to have a great relationship with God is by spending time alone with Him. As with any good "date" this exercise will require some planning. But make sure that you complete this sometime this week because it will be important as you move into the next section of the workbook. The following is our suggested format for your day in prayer. Some people also choose to make it a day of fasting in addition to a day of prayer. If you feel led to do this, you may find the experience to be rewarding.

WHERE'S YOUR FOCUS?: WEEK THREE — CARING FOR SELF

1. **Preparation:** Choose a quiet setting away from home. Consider going to a favorite fishing spot, a beautiful scenic setting, or a private get-a-way. Try to stay away from anything that would create undue financial and family stress. If you can afford it, an overnight trip would be fine. Bring your Bible, notebook or prayer journal, a praise book and a daily devotional.

2. **Morning:** Get an early start. Use the first portion of the day to thank God for everything that comes to mind. Include things such as the beauty surrounding you. Spend most of your morning just praising Him, using your praise book and devotional to help keep you focused. If you have a commentary, look up words such as love, prayer, and forgiveness. During the last part of the morning just be silent before God, and listen as He speaks to your heart.

3. **Afternoon:** Ask God to reveal to you the ways in which you have offended others. Make a list of the people that you need to approach and ask forgiveness. This is a very important part of your day with God because He warns us about coming to the altar when we have offenses against our brother (see Matthew 5: 23-24).

While thinking about your spouse, ask God for special understanding about the part you played in the status of your marital struggles. While you may not be the one who wants to separate or divorce, it is still important to ask God to reveal your sin, failures and shortcomings. Throughout the day, God may bring people to your mind that you may have offended; write their names down in order to take care of the situation when you return home.

4. **Evening:** Spend the evening looking at all the areas of your life that need to be changed in order for you to be in line with God's Word and His desires for you. In the case of sinful behavior or lifestyle, make a commitment to God to make those changes when you return. In situations such as: getting out of debt, reconciling with others, getting your body or health back in shape, or making changes that will impact others, set realistic time lines. Ask God to help you to be patient as you obey Him in the areas over which you have control. A balanced life is one that pleases God and glorifies Him as others look to you as an example of Christianity. More than likely it will be more enjoyable for you too. It also can be one of the factors that will rebuild your spouse's respect towards you.

After your day in prayer you will have a better understanding of your life and relationship with God and others. Make a point to approach those whom you have offended and begin the process of reconciliation. In regards to your spouse, pray for God's timing. Because of deep marital hurt, it may take longer for you to apologize and then ask your spouse to forgive you. But it's important that you not wait too long. It's also important not to approach your spouse expecting that he/she will ask for forgiveness in return. Try to state simply that you want to ask their forgiveness and then listen for their reply. This isn't the time to debate or dig up all the past hurts. It is just a time to apologize and ask for forgiveness. Whatever the response, pray and remain humble (asking God to equip you with His strength), and continue to seek forgiveness. Remember, forgiveness is an undeserved gift, so demanding to be forgiven is

WHERE'S YOUR FOCUS?: WEEK THREE — CARING FOR SELF

never appropriate. If your spouse refuses to forgive you, leave peacefully with the understanding that more time is needed *(Romans 12:18)*.

Reconciliation Tool 3B
"The Spiritual Fuel Tank Indicator"

Learning to focus on God in the midst of stressful circumstances takes practice. A "Spiritual Fuel Tank Indicator" can be a useful tool to assist the learning process.

When circumstances become stressful and feelings of uneasiness come over you, what is your first response? If you're like most, you'll probably do whatever you can to create peace in your life. Even though the desire for peace is good, if it is pursued without the benefit of God's guidance, the desire for "peace at any cost" can actually lead you astray and into sinful behavior. In the end, anything but peace is achieved.

Below is a tool that can help keep you focused in the right direction when you feel the first signs of uneasiness. Study the "spiritual fuel tank indicator" and notice that if you move the gauge arrow to the left of uneasiness, you will move into self-will, then into ungodly acts and eventually on "E," as you've eased God out of the situation.

However, if you choose prayer at the first signs of uneasiness you will engage the supernatural power of God. If your prayer is for God's direction and you then listen for His response, He will give you the wisdom to discern His guidance through the Holy Spirit, and eventually into "F". God's desire is for you to be full, and He is interested in helping you get there. As you allow Him to lead, He will help you discover how to become well cared for and full of His love. As you practice consistently focusing on God and going to Him in prayer when things are stressful, it will become a habit and you will be able to consistently make wise decisions in all areas of your life.

WHERE'S YOUR FOCUS?: WEEK THREE — CARING FOR SELF

WEEK THREE DISCUSSION QUESTIONS

Bring your journal from your day with God to discuss with your support partner anything significant that occurred in your heart. Also, read the following questions and write in your answers in order to discuss them with your support partner during your weekly meeting time.

■ **Open in prayer**

1. Describe any significant experiences or thoughts you had on your date with God.

2. How do you typically respond when you experience what feels like "God's silence" or an "unanswered prayer request?"

3. Were you able to reconcile with anyone whom God brought to your mind this week? How did you feel about asking that person for forgiveness, and how did they respond?

4. Were you able to identify some areas in your life that are out of balance, and, if so, how do you plan to become more balanced?

5. Are there some areas that are out of balance in your life over which you have very little control? What are they?

6. What is your impression of the focus meter? Where do you usually get stuck?

7. What has God shown you in His Word this week (Proverbs or other)?

8. Share any additional thoughts, insights from the Lord, or experiences that have happened this week that challenged your thinking or impacted your heart.

9. What is one thing that you are thankful for, and what is one concern to pray about.

■ **Close in prayer**

NOTES

WEEK FOUR

Valuing Differences

Do you want the freedom to be who you are?

From Joe: When Michelle and I first got back together after being separated for two years, we were both really happy and got along great. Then, after about two months, some of the same problems we'd had before began to surface. But this time we had both changed, and we had a commitment in the marriage we'd never had before. One of the changes was that we no longer used the words separation or divorce in our vocabulary. I knew that we would stay together, but I wanted there to be more than just commitment. I wanted joy and happiness in our marriage. I knew that God intended for marriage to be enjoyable, and I was determined not to let the little irritations in life destroy our ability to have fun in the marriage.

From Michelle: When Joe told me that he wanted more for our marriage than commitment, and that he wanted joy and happiness, I agreed, but I was at a loss as to how to accomplish it. Our old habits and ways of doing things were so much a part of who we were, and both of us had the idea that the other one was doing it wrong. Joe was determined to put fun into our marriage and I was goal-driven and wanted us to accomplish things. Then, one Sunday we happened to see some tapes on the different temperament styles, and it changed our marriage and home life forever.

Joe and Michelle finally understood that neither was wrong. God actually designed them with their own temperament style and with unique differences. After taking a temperament test they began to understand each other's strengths and weaknesses. They were able to see each other in a whole new light and began to actually appreciate their God given differences. In fact, it brought so much new joy to their marriage because they realized that they really weren't trying to irritate each other. Rather, they were just wired differently.

"The Temperament Profile"

On the next two pages you will find a simple paper/pencil test to help you identify your basic temperament. As far back as the Greek philosopher, Hippocrates, people have been fascinated with obvious unique differences of individual personality types. In the past decade well-known Christian authors and speakers such as Fred and Florence Littauer, Gary Smalley and John Trent, and Tim and Beverly LaHaye have written and lectured on the four basic temperaments. While some of them refer to each one with different titles, the best known are the ones coined by Hippocrates: Sanguine (outgoing), Choleric (leader), Melancholy (perfectionist), and Phlegmatic (peacemaker).

Even if you have taken a temperament profile in the past, make the time to take it again. Sometimes, because of stressful circumstances and trying to please your spouse, you can mask who you really are. Because you have been spending time in God's Word the past three weeks, and have been getting your focus off your spouse to meet his/her needs or have him/her meet yours, your results will be more accurate.

WHERE'S YOUR FOCUS?: WEEK FOUR— VALUING DIFFERENCES

For those of you who love this sort of thing and either want to go further into understanding your and your spouse's personality differences and would like to take a user-friendly computerized personality profile, consider the *Personality Profile for Couples*. It is based on the Enneagram; a personality test that has been in existence for centuries. This profile captures even more of the subtle differences between us all and classifies people into 9 basic personality types instead of just 4. If you take this test with your spouse, it will identify both personalities and then provide you with a 5-9 page detailed report outlining the strengths and weaknesses of each personality. To order a version of this fascinating personality instrument, go to our website at www.nationalmarriage.com and in the resources section, order the Personality Profile for Couples.

TEMPERAMENT PROFILE
Reconciling God's Way Ministries

After studying the four choices across, please circle the word or sentence that best or most often describes you. You will probably identify with all to a degree, but circle only the one that best applies. If you are not sure, ask someone who knows you well.

Strengths

1.	Full of life	Risk taker	Analytical	Adapts to any situation
2.	Playful	Convincing	Finishes projects	Easy-going
3.	Social	Head-strong	Self-sacrificing	Accepts others rules
4.	Funny	Commanding	Reliable	Friendly
5.	Cheerful	Self-assured	Artistic	Even-tempered
6.	Talkative	Goal-oriented	Thoughtful	Tolerant
7.	Lively	Leader	Loyal	Good listener
8.	Inspiring	Independent	Expects perfection	Agreeable
9.	Optimistic	Outspoken	Organized	Accommodating

Subtotal your scores by adding the amount of each column, and go on to the next page.

_____   _____   _____   _____

Developed by **Reconciling God's Way** Ministries

WHERE'S YOUR FOCUS?: WEEK FOUR— VALUING DIFFERENCES

Weaknesses

10.	Undisciplined	Unsympathetic	Holds grudges	Lazy
11.	Interrupts	Impatient	Never good enough	Indecisive
12.	Too talkative	Inconsiderate	Easily offended	Peace at any cost
13.	Naive	Overly confident	Negative	Unconcerned
14.	Disorganized	Controlling	Depressed	Lack of confidence
15.	Messy	Shrewd	Moody	Mumbles
16.	Loud	Domineering	Avoids people	Too tired to work
17.	Short attention span	Critical/judgmental	Manipulative	Too compromising
18.	Inconsistent	Intolerant	Introvert	Indifferent

_____ _____ _____ _____

Strengths (from previous page).

_____ _____ _____ _____

Grand totals

_____ _____ _____ _____

Developed By Reconciling God's Way Ministries

Temperament Types Answer Sheet

After you have totaled all your answers, the column with the highest number will identify your temperament. The descriptions below are a summary of each temperament.

Column One: *Expressives* (Otter or Sanguine)

WHERE'S YOUR FOCUS?: WEEK FOUR— VALUING DIFFERENCES

This personality type lives life to the fullest. They are carefree, and love to bring life and laughter to any group setting. People are usually drawn to their optimistic attitude and to their exuberant energy. The "Expressives" like to be involved in many things, and are very comfortable being the center of attention. Lack of discipline and organization can be a downfall to this type, especially if they work or live in an environment where organization and discipline are valued by others.

Column Two: *Drivers* (Lion or Choleric)

This personality type loves a challenge. They are natural leaders, and are very strong personality types. They are goal-oriented and driven toward success. They are self-assured and convincing, and people follow them. The "Drivers" have to be careful not to run over other people's thoughts and feelings. Insensitivity can be a downfall.

Column Three: *Analyticals* (Beaver or Melancholy)

This is the perfectionist type. The "Analyticals" are detail-oriented and organized. They work hard at doing things right. The Analyticals also tend to be black and white thinkers (things are right or wrong, with very little grey).They have high standards for themselves, but need to be careful not to impose those standards on others. Their weakness might be in the area of being critical or judgmental.

Column Four: *Amiables* (Golden Retriever or Phlegmatic)

This is the peacemaker personality type. The Amiables don't like conflict and err on the side of "peace at any cost." They are warm, friendly and caring people whom others enjoy being around. Their downside is usually in the area of laziness, or losing who they are in order to please others.

Remember that God created us in His image, and that Jesus' personality was perfectly balanced. While we are not (and never will be) perfect, we are to strive for a healthy balance in our behavior.

Read the strengths of the temperaments in which you scored low, and stretch yourself whenever possible to implement some of those strengths in your life. Look over the strengths of yourself and your mate, and try as often as you can to be thankful for those strengths, and use them for the glory of God!

In the scoring of your temperament profile, you will probably find that you have two temperaments that are close in number, with the other two much lower. That's common, but there are those who just score very high in one temperament and low in the other three. If you score evenly in three or all four, take the test again and ask someone who knows you well to

WHERE'S YOUR FOCUS?: WEEK FOUR— VALUING DIFFERENCES

help you in your answers, in order to end up with your highest scores in no more than two columns. After you have taken your test, take the test again with different colored ink to find your spouse's temperament.

The purpose of identifying your own temperament, as well as your spouse's, is not to label others or give excuses for negative behavior. It is meant to generate understanding and appreciation of each other. When Joe and Michelle began to understand each other, it changed their interpersonal responses. Along with increased understanding, improved responses led to a greater sense of joy in their family. They went to their five children (his, hers, and theirs) and sincerely let them know that they appreciated each one's uniqueness. They also realized through watching some personality videos that a temperament strength pushed to extreme becomes a weakness. That knowledge helped them not to be so harsh on each other when one of them was exhibiting a weakness.

If you are able to spend some time with your spouse this week, go over the temperament tests together and compare your answers. Use the time to discuss the list of strengths of each of your temperaments, rather than the weaknesses. Focusing on the strengths of your mate's temperament tends to encourage him/her to exhibit those strengths in your marriage. If you are separated or if your mate is unwilling to take and discuss the test, you can still look over the list of strengths with the purpose of understanding what your spouse is capable of bringing into the marriage.

Reconciliation Tool 4A
"Focus On Your Mate's Good Qualities"

Get a package of 3x5 cards and for the next 8 weeks plan on using one card daily. On your card each day (preferably during your daily quiet time) make a list of all the qualities that are positive in your spouse. If you have to remember back to your dating days, that's okay. If your spouse did something kind for you or one of your children, write it down. If they paid a bill, worked on your car, kept a commitment, or just said a kind word, make a note of it.

Jot down anything at all that comes to mind regarding the good qualities in your mate. Remember that everyone has strengths and weaknesses, and it's impossible for anyone not to have some good qualities. It is possible, however, for people to miss the good qualities because of focusing on the negative all the time.

You may find this exercise difficult to do for a couple of reasons. (I) You have probably not been used to thinking of your mate's good qualities because of past and present hurts, and (2) If you don't like to write, it will take discipline to write daily. But, this exercise is a very important part of the reconciliation process because it takes practice to get into the habit of changing the way you think about your spouse. If you write these positive traits down regularly, you will begin to change your thinking, and subsequently change your behavior toward your spouse. If you want to reconcile God's way, He commands that you love one another and not harbor bitterness. No matter how your spouse is behaving at the present time, do this exercise with all

WHERE'S YOUR FOCUS?: WEEK FOUR— VALUING DIFFERENCES

the determination you can muster. Trust God to give you the insight you need to focus on the positive!

WHERE'S YOUR FOCUS?: WEEK FOUR— VALUING DIFFERENCES

Reconciliation Tool 4B
"Verbally Compliment Your Mate"

The best way to put joy in your marriage is to verbally compliment one another. Even in situations where couples are separated we have seen miracles happen just because the conversation between them changed from negative comments to positive ones. This last exercise in the Focus section of the workbook is one of the most important tools you will use in reconciling. Family members and friends need to hear you saying kind things about the person you are married to, not to mention that your spouse needs to hear it. This tool is for the benefit of everyone with whom you come in contact, including your spouse.

Make it a point to verbally compliment your spouse to his/her face or to someone else at least twice a day. Researchers have said that it takes five positive comments to erase one negative one, so if you really want to make a difference, do more. Due to the 5:1 positive to negative interaction ratio, the job of positively rebuilding your marriage is made easier by also limiting the number of negative comments. Each negative comment you make means you need to come up with five more positive. The habit of speaking positively about and to one another will be very important as we move into the next section of the workbook and you continue to work on reconciling.

From Joe: *Before I learned about the temperaments and understood that Michelle's main temperament was choleric, I couldn't understand why she was always so driven to get things accomplished. I used to say to her, "Just lighten up! Have a little fun in life! We don't always have to be setting some new goal to reach some new accomplishment!" I also thought that she was always trying to control everything because she liked being in leadership positions. The one thing that saved us, I think, was that her second strongest temperament is sanguine (which is my first strongest), and so there was enough spontaneity and fun in her that we had that in common. Now I don't get irritated with her when she's setting goals and serving in leadership positions-I see it as a strength and not as a threat.*

From Michelle: *I always wondered why Joe wanted to wear bright colored ties and drive cars that created so much attention. I used to think, can't he just be "beige" and blend in with others? Does he always have to stand out and be so noticeable? I not only tried to tell him how to dress, but I also tried to make him more driven in the area of goals and accomplishments. I would say things like, "What do you mean you want to go for a drive? The lawn needs mowing, or we should be preparing for whatever goal 'we' were working towards)." Now and then, when I would be in my sanguine mode, I would be able to enjoy those spontaneous get-a-ways, instead of "work," but otherwise my strong desire to accomplish kept me from just "lightening up," as Joe would say. It wasn't until I learned about the sanguine temperament that I realized Joe's unique difference from me was the way God had designed him and that it was okay for him to not be so goal-oriented. I not only learned to appreciate his unique qualities, but was able to enjoy life more because I understood that God had created everyone with strengths and weaknesses to complement one another, rather than compete. Thankfully, Joe's second strongest temperament happens to be choleric, so we are able to accomplish quite a bit as a*

WHERE'S YOUR FOCUS?: WEEK FOUR— VALUING DIFFERENCES

team. I have to watch, however, that I stay Christ-centered and balanced in order to not push him (and us) into too many activities. His ability to say no to me has helped us in this area.

WEEK FOUR DISCUSSION QUESTIONS

Read the following questions and write in your answers in order to discuss them with your support partner during your weekly meeting time:

■ **Open in prayer**

1. What are your two strongest temperaments/traits?

2. What are the strongest temperaments/traits in the rest of your family (and spouse)?

3. What strengths do you exhibit most frequently? What about your spouse?

4. What weaknesses do you struggle with most?

5. Were you able to verbally compliment your spouse? Were you able to compliment someone else?

6. What has God shown you this week in your study of Proverbs?

7. Share any additional thoughts, insights from the Lord, or experiences that have happened this week that challenged your thinking or impacted your heart.

8. What is one thing you are thankful for this week? What concern can your support partner pray for this week?

■ **Close in prayer**

NOTES

SECTION TWO

WHERE'S YOUR HEART?
The secrets in your heart are powerful predictors of present and future pain.

"Search me, 0 God, and know my heart; test me and know my anxious thoughts"(Psalm 139:23).

WEEK FIVE

Secret Motives
Do you really want to reconcile?

When actors are on stage rehearsing their lines for a play, oftentimes the director will walk by and call out *"subtext."* The director wants to know from the actors if they understand the underlying theme of the play and if they really know the meaning of their lines. For instance, if the actors are supposed to be in love, their body language and the way they deliver their lines should show that. The audience would be confused if the lines were delivered in a tone of voice and body movements that contradicted the subtext (or subplot) of the play.

> **So, what's your subtext? Do you really want reconciliation in your marriage?**

From Joe: *There were times during our separation when Michelle would tell me one thing, but act like she meant another. For instance, sometimes she would tell me that she missed me and say she wanted me to move back home, and then she would become angry and distant soon afterwards. When that would happen I'd get defensive and assume that she'd changed her mind. There were other times that her words and actions didn't line up concerning our relationship, and it just caused me a lot of frustration because I felt like I had to second-guess her.*

From Michelle: *As I mentioned before, when Joe and I finally separated-after years of arguing-I was actually relieved. Things were finally peaceful at home, but I did miss the good times in our marriage and I missed being a wife and homemaker (not to mention wanting to do God's will in my life). So when I would tell Joe I missed him and wanted to reconcile, that was partly true, but not completely. I was fearful for us to move back together, and had many concerns I didn't want to have to deal with, one of which was my loss of respect and love for him.*

I didn't know how to discuss my fears and my feelings with him, so I would withdraw or lash out in anger at the least little thing. Consequently, it took us much longer than it would have to actually move back in together.

If you are separated from your spouse, or if your marriage is hanging on by a thread, you are going to have to come to terms with some tough questions. Reconciliation takes a lot of work, time, and commitment. After Joe and Michelle had been separated for a year and a half, they met with a pastor at their church for six weeks, and did nothing but argue in his office each week. They really hadn't attended counseling for the purpose of working things out. Instead neither of them wanted to be the one who said no when the pastor requested a meeting with them. This scenario is not uncommon. After they reconciled and began holding classes for couples going through the same struggle, they observed couples come to class with folded arms and downcast faces. There was no observable desire to follow the guidelines for reconciling. Each person seemed to show up to class so it could be said they had "tried".

WHERE'S YOUR HEART?: WEEK FIVE — SECRET MOTIVES

> **The good news is God can even use wrong motive to reveal His Truths.**

From Michelle: *Concerning our counseling situation, the funny thing is that the whole six weeks that we sat in that pastor's office arguing, God used it to allow me to bring all my fears and issues out in the open, which ultimately saved our marriage! I had never felt free to tell Joe all the reasons I didn't think we could reconcile. I guess I didn't want to deal with his reactions (I often would keep my real feelings inside even with others because I didn't want a negative response from them). So, in that office I just got it all out. Sometimes the pastor left us alone to argue while he waited out in the hall (looking back, I laugh at that now), so it wasn't necessarily that I felt safer with a third party present. It was that I finally took the risk to get everything out in the open with the probability that Joe would get so fed up that he would just file for divorce and I'd be free.*

I know that doesn't sound very "Christian" of me, but my feelings for Joe had died by then. I really didn't think I loved him anymore. I just couldn't believe that God would want me to be married to someone I didn't love, and I felt trapped because of my Christian beliefs.

From Joe: *I knew that there were behaviors that I would need to change if our marriage was really going to work. When Michelle finally took a hard stand with me, even though I didn't like what I heard, it actually helped me because I knew that she wasn't going to "let" me get away with behavior I shouldn't be doing anyway. One time I heard someone say, "You choose to do what you choose to do," and I guess I finally came to an understanding that if I were ever going to be the man God had intended for me to be, it had to start with my making the right choices. Eventually I was thankful that Michelle had finally been honest with her fears. We actually moved back in together a couple months later.*

Sometimes you or your spouse will send confusing messages about reconciling because of a natural inner conflict. The inner conflict often centers on the desire to love/be loved and the great risk required to achieve that. Rather than accepting, understanding and acknowledging the inner conflict, a person will try to deny one or both sides of the conflict. In doing so, the conflicted spouse's feelings are neglected and the other spouse is never fully informed. In the end the opportunity for change is lost.

Reconciliation Tool 5A
"Ask Tough Questions"

Regardless of your situation or motives for going through this workbook, this exercise is very important. Depending on how long your relationship has been stressed, you have both been living in a situation that is difficult. In stressful situations it is tempting to want to be free from the pain, even if it means going against God's Will and His Word. Pray before you begin this exercise and answer the following questions:

1. List 5-10 reasons why you want your marriage to stay together:

WHERE'S YOUR FOCUS?: WEEK FIVE—SECRET MOTIVES

2. List any reason at all that comes to mind as to why you might be afraid to stay with your spouse (this would include any immoral behavior going on either on your behalf or your spouse's, i.e., adultery, drugs or alcohol, abuse of you or children, pornography, etc.) Please be honest in this section. If you are concerned about writing in this workbook, write in code that only you would understand, or use a separate sheet of paper and throw it away after this exercise is completed. If your spouse is involved in any immoral behavior and refuses to repent, you will need to address that separately. A pastor or Christian counselor who is skilled in how to set up healthy relationship boundaries can help guide you.

3. In what ways have you sent mixed or confusing messages to your spouse about your intent to reconcile?

After looking over the three previous questions and prayerfully asking God to give you wisdom, study the Scriptures listed and write what your own thoughts are concerning the verse:

'Therefore, if anyone is in Christ, he is a new creation; the old has gone, the new has come" (2 Corinthians 5:17).

Thoughts:

"If anyone thinks he is something when he is nothing, he deceives himself" (Galatians 6:3).

Thoughts:

WHERE'S YOUR HEART?: WEEK FIVE — SECRET MOTIVES

"Blessed is the man who perseveres under trial, because when he has stood the test, he will receive the crown of life that God has promised to those who love Him" (James 1:12).

Thoughts:

'No temptation has seized you except what is common to man. And God is faithful; He will not let you be tempted beyond what you can bear. But when you are tempted, He will also provide a way out so that you can stand up under it" (1 Corinthians 10:13).

Thoughts:

"For this reason a man will leave his father and mother and be united to his wife, and the two will become one flesh" (Ephesians 5:31).

Thoughts:

"Therefore each of you must put off falsehood and speak truthfully to his neighbor, for we are all members of one body" (Ephesians 4:25).

Thoughts:

One final thought: While we are not actors on stage rehearsing our lines for a play, it would probably do many of us well at times to imagine God (the great Director of our lives) calling out to us. "Subtext," and our saying back to Him, "Your will, and not mine, Lord."

WEEK FIVE DISCUSSION QUESTIONS

Read the following questions and write in your answers in order to discuss them with your support partner during your weekly meeting time:

■ **Open in prayer**

1. Share your answer to Reconciliation Tool 5A. What are the reasons you want to reconcile?

2. Share your answers as to what you fear about reconciling?

3. If the Holy Spirit convicted you this past week in a particular area, please share it with your support partner. It will be important for you to bring it to light and make a commitment to be held accountable for the remainder of your time together.

4. Share your answers from the Scriptures that you studied this week. Which one was most meaningful?

5. In your study of Proverbs this week, what did God show you?

6. Share any additional thoughts, insights from the Lord, or experiences that have happened this week that challenged your thinking or impacted your heart.

7. Share with your support partner one thing that you are thankful for and one concern for which you need prayer.

■ **Close in prayer.**

NOTES

WEEK SIX

Secret Anger

Understand your anger....revolutionize your marriage!

We have noticed that many marriages in crisis have a common misunderstanding of anger. Most couples openly admit that they either fear their mate's raging anger or are frustrated because their mate clams up and refuses to admit they are angry at all. All through the Bible, God expressed His own anger at Israel and all those who disobeyed Him. In the New Testament Jesus expressed His anger at the Pharisees more than once. Since we were created in God's image *(Genesis 1:27)*, and God expressed anger, then we know that it is a natural emotion.

Neil Clark Warren, in his book, *Make Anger Your Ally*, explains that there are four basic reasons we become angry: (1) Fear (2) Frustration (3) Hurt (4) Injustice. In intimate relationships it's no wonder there are anger issues to deal with constantly. The broad use of the term "anger" can lead to great misunderstanding. For instance, one can conclude a spouse's anger is meant to induce hurt when in reality it was an attempt to express the spouse's hurt.

If we have to live with the emotion of anger and the triggers are all around, is there any hope of ever having harmony in our home? We believe the answer is yes. If there was ever a couple who had anger issues and used sinful behaviors as a form of expression, it was the Williams. Joe and Michelle were raised without knowing the Lord. Both had expressive temperaments. Therefore, the way they communicated anger left a lot to be desired. When they began following Christ, they chose to change lifestyles in order to attempt to be more caring and godly in how they treated each other. But they quickly discovered that one of the most difficult areas for them to master was the area of anger. They often struggled with knowing how to be angry without sinning, as the Bible commands *(Eph. 4:26)*.

From Joe: *When Michelle would get angry with me I never knew what to expect. Sometimes she'd break something. Other times she'd say things that I couldn't believe could come out of her mouth. Not long into our marriage I just got used to the idea that if we had a blow-up over something, anything was liable to happen, so I would try as hard as I could to keep her from getting mad. Then, when I'd least expect it, wham! I'd say something that triggered some feeling or thought, and she'd explode. All three times we separated (two short ones before our two-year split), it was right after one of those big explosions.*

From Michelle: *When I disagreed with things that Joe said and did, and would tell him my feelings, he'd get so irritated with me that I just got into the habit of not saying anything. As I said earlier, I felt a lot of pressure to keep him happy and show him he was loved, and that put me in a position of feeling like I couldn't really be honest. I also didn't know how to handle situations when Joe would make choices that I didn't like and in my desire to keep peace and have things run smoothly at home, I just stuffed my feelings. Then, as Joe explained, when he least expected it, over some trivial matter, I'd blow. It took me a long time to understand that I was not responsible for Joe's reactions, and I had a responsibility to be respectfully honest, regardless.*

WHERE'S YOUR HEART?: WEEK SIX — SECRET ANGER

It took the Williams years to learn what was shared with you in the above story. They knew, from teaching it to many couples, that if you will faithfully practice the techniques we're giving you and understand the purpose behind them (along with next week's lesson on honesty), your marriage will be revolutionized. Even if your spouse chooses not to participate, your changed behavior will absolutely affect the way you both communicate from now on.

Reconciliation Tool 6A
"Identify Your Choice Of Expression"

In *Make Anger Your Ally*, Neil Clark Warren identifies four main techniques that people commonly use when dealing with anger. They are each listed on the next page. As you go through the list rate them in order of #1-4, with #1 being the technique you choose most. Then, next to your rating, put what you believe to be your spouse's. Notice that they are all negative responses, so even though we are asking you to take a moment to rate your spouse, the purpose of this exercise is to identify similarities and differences in style. Make sure your primary focus and attention remains on your use of anger. We'll give you some tools for positive responses later on.

Rate _____

1. **Exploder:** People who explode never have ulcers (but everyone around them does!) Exploders use their aggressive behavior (yelling, slamming things, physical altercations, etc.) to intimidate and control others.

Rate _____

2. **Somatizer:** This person pretends that everything is fine when it isn't. They don't look angry, but inside they are in knots. They have headaches, colitis, stomach problems and unidentified illnesses. Possibly the only time they ever got attention as children was when they were ill.

Rate _____

3. **Self-Punisher:** This person has turned his/her anger in on themselves. They are usually perfectionists, and because they aren't "perfect" they become frustrated. Consequently, most of them struggle with depression. Sadness, withdrawal and self-blame are ongoing in their lives.

Rate _____

4. **Underhandler:** Judas was an underhandler in his dealings with Jesus and the disciples. This person pretends to be your friend, but in reality is coming in through the back door as your enemy. They don't have many close friends and are gossips and backbiters. They

WHERE'S YOUR HEART?: WEEK SIX — SECRET ANGER

also tend to be passive-aggressive. It is suggested that people who choose to express their anger in this method were not allowed to show any anger expression at home while growing up.

Reconciliation Tool 6B
"Identify Your Anger"

Get another pack of 3x5 cards, (or small note pad) and carry them with you this whole week. Every time you feel the emotion of anger, and you start to express it by one of the four choices, jot it down. Write whether you were **frustrated, fearful, hurt** (emotionally or physically), or experienced an **injustice** (yourself or someone else's).And yes, you can experience a couple or even all four at once. This is an important step because you will begin to see a pattern for what makes you angry, and that will come in handy in the next step.

Reconciliation Tool 6C
"Bring It to the Light"

This is where making honesty, especially with yourself, more important than your fear of other's thoughts and opinions. Being honest with what you are feeling will help you to bring anger issues to the light and not let Satan have a foothold *(Ephesians 4: 27)*. Being real with your mate (if this can be done without exposing you to physical danger), can give your relationship a foundation of honesty to stand upon. This last tool of the week will take much practice, so don't get discouraged. Your assignment is to just grasp the concept, and practice it as much as you possibly can.

1. **The next time you feel anger, say so out loud and identify exactly why you are angry.** For instance, if you are frustrated because you can't find something and it's causing you to be late for an appointment, say, 'I'm really frustrated right now because I can't find (my keys) and it's making me late." It is critically important here to learn how to express your anger without blaming. Notice how different saying, 'I'm really frustrated right now," sounds from, 'You make me so frustrated." The first one is you owning your feelings and taking responsibility for them, the second is blaming someone else and trying to get them to take responsibility. At first it will be hard enough for your spouse to hear without reacting to. However, the second one will almost always evoke a defensive response.

2. **Then, after identifying your reason aloud, pray aloud for God to give you supernatural strength and wisdom not to sin in your frustration (anger).** If it's another person triggering your frustration, identify out loud to the person that you are feeling frustrated (they know it anyway), but do not use the word "angry"—keep it to the issue of "frustration," (or fear, injustice, or hurt).This is crucial for learning to express anger without sinning, and it truly will bring a new respect to you and others once it's learned. The reason for not using the word "anger" in dealing with the other person is because the word itself is so emotionally charged, it often feels threatening. The person listening will typically become defensive as soon as they hear it, especially when it is attached to blame. But the words "fear",

WHERE'S YOUR HEART?: WEEK SIX — SECRET ANGER

"frustration", "hurt", and "injustice" are emotions with which people can more easily identify, and thus are more likely to diffuse any defensive reactions.

If it's inappropriate to pray aloud in the moment, God can hear your silent plea to Him and He will give you the strength and wisdom not to sin in your anger. But you must ask and believe (see *James 1: 5-6*).

3. **The final step in this last tool is to confess your own contribution to the situation.** If there is anything you need to confess, do it. Once you ask God to give you the wisdom you need, He will show you your part in the situation. There is almost always a way we contribute something even if it is only towards the intensity of our emotions and the way we express them. It is important that you not get into the habit of thinking that every situation that causes you to feel angry is always someone else's fault. In fact, if you usually see your negative feelings as primarily caused by others, you will typically see others as both the problem and the solution. Making yourself feel better then becomes dependent on the other person changing or doing something. The resulting feelings of powerlessness and dependence on someone you can't control will tend to make you even more frustrated and angry!

From Michelle: *For the first couple of years after we reconciled I read everything I could get my hands on concerning anger. I listened to well-known authors and speakers, and I studied God's Word on the subject of anger. As I began to see changes in my life by putting much of the information I'd learned into practice, I felt a real sense of freedom. I no longer was afraid of anger, and it wasn't a lurking monster waiting to devour me anymore. Anger really was my friend. I knew God had given me the emotion of anger to help me identify things I needed to change in my life. I finally understood that getting my feelings out in the open, and allowing God to give me His supernatural strength to change me, was also allowing those around me to change. When I began to have self-control in my anger, and not sin in it, Joe had to deal with the real issue at hand, instead of what either of us did while angry. I know now that Satan likes us to get side-tracked by our sinful behavior instead of dealing with the real issues that caused the anger, because dealing with the issues builds strong marriages!*

From Joe: When Michelle stopped having those anger explosions it took me about a year to finally believe it. I would think to myself, "I know it's coming, she's gonna blow any day now." And she wouldn't. Our marriage is so different now because neither of us worries about what the other one is going to do in their anger. We also understand that even if one of us sins in our anger it's between that person and God, and that the other one needs to practice personal self-control no matter what. (We don't have those major explosions anymore, but we do slip up and say or do things at times that are still hurtful.)

When we teach on anger, I like to use the example of a hand grenade. I use an old one (diffused, of course) and that we have mounted like a trophy and I call it an "angernade." I hold it up and tell the people that we are all potential "angernades" if we are not expressing our anger properly and getting in the light. If we are stuffing it or pretending it's not there, rest assured, the damage will occur eventually, and casualties will sadly result.

WHERE'S YOUR HEART?: WEEK SIX — SECRET ANGER

The good news is that although negative, and sometimes even sinful, behaviors for expressing anger are learned, through practice and understanding these expressions can be . Changing the way Joe and Michelle dealt with anger not only revolutionized their marriage, but it helped them deal with other relationships as well. They also have been able to share these important tools with their children and grandchildren to encourage them to form healthy habits for dealing with the emotion of anger.

WEEK SIX DISCUSSION QUESTIONS

Read the following questions and write in your answers in order to discuss them with your support partner during your weekly meeting time:

 Open in prayer

1. After reading about the different ways people express anger, how did you rate yourself?

2. Did you track what made you angry this week? If not, why? If so, do you want to share a couple of situations with your support partner?

3. Did you tell anyone this week that you were frustrated, fearful, hurt, or felt an injustice? If so, explain how it took place and what happened afterwards.

4. What did God show you this week concerning Proverbs?

5. Share any additional thoughts, insights from the Lord, or experiences that have happened this week that have challenged your thinking or impacted your heart.

6. Tell your support partner one thing he/she can be in prayer for this week, and give one praise report. You have made it half way through the workbook. As you close in prayer this week, ask God to help you complete your commitment.

 Close in prayer

NOTES

WEEK SEVEN

Secret Lies

Honesty is at the core of true intimacy.

If there is one thing that will sabotage intimacy in marriage, it's dishonesty. If either of you has a problem being honest, it will commonly be more difficult for you to control your anger in a healthy way and deal with the areas in your marriage that need strengthening. Willard Harley, in his book His Needs, Her Needs, suggests there are three basic reasons why people are dishonest in their marriage: (1) **to protect others**, (2) **to avoid trouble**, and (3) **to lie for no reason (chronic lying).**

We've added one more reason: **to control**. In our own marriage and in many of the couples we've counseled, the desire to control circumstances, other people, and each other can be a constant source of "little white lying" in the home. It took us a long time to realize that controlling circumstances by twisting the facts, not telling because they weren't asked, and leaving out details in order to get the desired results, was just plain lying, and God calls it sin.

From Michelle: *I remember a time when I thought I had overdrawn our business checking account. I was so afraid of Joe's reaction that I called my grandfather and borrowed the money from him without telling Joe. A few months later, after paying the money back, I realized that I had read the statement wrong, and I had to explain the extra money in the account. Instead of Joe being happy that we had some extra money, he was furious. He could only wonder how many other times I had "helped" a situation he should have known about. There were so many times that I hid things for the sake of keeping peace, or I would manipulate situations so that things would turn out like I wanted them to. I didn't consider it dishonesty; I just considered it "little white lies" and believed ends justified the means.*

From Joe: *The problem I had in the area of dishonesty was that I wouldn't tell Michelle what I was really thinking, and I would keep things from her that I thought would cause conflict. We both had a problem with second-guessing each other and assuming that we knew what the other's response was going to be in various circumstances. When we thought the response was going to be negative, it was just easier to avoid the discussion altogether. After we reconciled and began working on not second-guessing each other, it would really bother me when Michelle treated me with that old "assuming" attitude and didn't give me the opportunity to show her I'd changed.*

A couple years after Joe and Michelle reconciled, they realized that when certain situations came up, they were still relating to each other based on old behaviors. Dishonesty and mistrust between them were issues that had caused a lot of arguing and pain. They knew that God wanted them to be truthful in all circumstances. Each time they took a step of faith and chose to be honest (even when they feared the other's response) their intimacy level rose to new heights.

WHERE'S YOUR HEART?: WEEK SEVEN — SECRET LIES

LOW RISK = LOW INTIMACY

HIGH RISK - HIGH INTIMACY

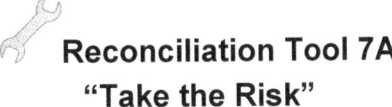

Reconciliation Tool 7A
"Take the Risk"

In last week's lesson you were asked to identify what were the core emotions fueling feelings of anger. This week we want to ask you to identify the reasons you are not totally honest with your mate. Remember, this is not just about telling lies; it's about withholding information, twisting facts, and manipulating circumstances as well.

1. **Identify which area you tend to struggle with the most when it comes to being dishonest, and rate them in order (mark 1 for the one you struggle with the most and 4 for the one you struggle with the least).**

Protecting (you want to keep others from suffering consequences or pain)

Rate _____

Avoiding trouble (you fear others' reactions or rejection)

Rate _____

Chronic lying (you exaggerate or lie for no reason)

Rate _____

Controlling (you manipulate to get your way)

Rate _____

   Ask God to give you the supernatural strength you will need in order to obey Him the next time you are faced with having to be honest in a situation on that you'd rather be dishonest in.

2. **Then, look for an opportunity to practice taking the risk to be honest with your mate or anyone else that God puts in your path.** Once you decide to start practicing truth instead of dishonesty, you'll probably start seeing many areas in your life that you've not been honest

WHERE'S YOUR HEART?: WEEK SEVEN — SECRET LIES

in and had not even realized it. These days, "situational ethics" and being politically correct are so much a part of our world that it's easy to excuse dishonesty.

Reconciliation Tool 7B
"What Does God Say?"

Look up the following Scriptures and write in your own words what those Scripture verses say to you about the importance of honesty.

Ephesians 4:25

Colossians 3:9-10

Proverbs 14:5

Proverbs 12:22

Romans 16:17-19

I Corinthians 13:4-7

WEEK SEVEN DISCUSSION QUESTIONS

Read the following questions and write in your answers in order to discuss them with your support partner during your weekly meeting time:

 Open in prayer

1. Share how you rated yourself on the dishonesty scale. Explain your answer.

2. Did you always struggle with dishonesty in that way prior to marriage? If so, describe how this played out in other relationships or in childhood.

3. Did you have an opportunity this week to speak truth when you could have been dishonest? Please explain.

4. In your exercise this week on looking up verses in tool 7B, was there a verse that stood out to you on the issue of honesty?

5. Do you find that you tend to be fearful that your mate is not always being honest? List some reasons that tend to make you fearful of being honest in all circumstances (this will be helpful for next week too):

6. What was one thing that God showed you in your study of Proverbs this week?

7. Share any additional thoughts, insights from the Lord, or experiences that have happened this week that challenged your thinking or impacted your heart.

8. Have you been able to continue doing your nurture activities weekly? If not, what has prevented you from doing so?

9. Share with your support partner one thing that you are thankful for and one concern for him/her to pray about for you.

 Close in prayer.

NOTES

WEEK EIGHT

Secret Fears

What keeps you from being real with your mate?

Wrong motives, unresolved anger, and dishonesty are sins of the heart that will always create a wall of fear between a husband and wife and stop meaningful communication. While honesty is at the core of true intimacy, if either of you fears the other (emotionally or physically) it will be extremely difficult risk being honest. The issue of fear must be dealt with if the marriage is to survive and reconciliation is to take place.

From Joe: *There were so many times that I wanted to tell Michelle what I was frustrated about, or didn't want her doing, but I was afraid that it would cause her to leave me. I had convinced myself early in our marriage that I wasn't really enough for her and in looking back I can see how my fear of losing her to someone else kept me from being open and honest in my communication with her. I wouldn't even discuss my taste in clothes, cars, and homes because they were different than Michelle's, and I thought it was better to just keep my opinions to myself. Then, because I had all that frustration and fear bottled up inside, it came out every few months in behavior that almost destroyed our marriage.*

From Michelle: *For the first five years of our marriage, I felt as if I were walking on eggshells every time Joe was frustrated. I didn't understand it at the time, but my fear of his reactions kept me from saying and doing the things that would have helped build communication and intimacy between us. There were many times that I should have lovingly, but truthfully, confronted Joe when he had been disrespectful toward me. He should have done the same with me as well, instead of waiting until so much time had passed that I couldn't even remember the offense. Our fear of each other's reactions was not only causing communication problems for us, but it was also keeping us from being all that God had intended us to be. I loved when Joe finally started speaking from his heart and sharing his likes and dislikes with me, even if we disagreed. When we both began practicing biblical truths, our mutual respect grew quickly.*

Joe and Michelle heard a Christian speaker once say, concerning the emotion of fear, "Just do it afraid!" That may not be the best method to use if we feel unsafe with our spouse physically or emotionally. Safety in a marriage relationship is essential. A truly intimate connection always involves some type of a deep heart-to-heart sharing of who you are; a knowing and being known. If people are afraid of being hurt, opening their heart will be difficult at best and careless at worst. But feeling emotionally unsafe is *not only* related to how our spouse treats us. Some people struggle trusting anyone with access to the deeper places in their heart. Proverbs 4:23 states, "Above all else, guard your heart for it is the wellspring of life." In addition to not trusting others, a deeper fear results from not trusting yourself to know how to care for and protect your own heart. When the knowledge and skill required to "guard your heart" in an intimate encounter is missing, your emotional well-being is completely dependent on the other person; a vulnerable position indeed!

Consequently, you may never be able to experience deep intimacy because you refuse to risk ever really allowing your spouse access to your heart. It just feels too dangerous; too risky. As

WHERE'S YOUR HEART?: WEEK EIGHT — SECRET FEARS

a result, you will likely miss out on the possibility of enjoying the deep satisfaction of real intimacy.

However, a commitment to taking good care of your own heart, and developing the skill and confidence to do so, will make allowing someone access to your heart feel far less dangerous. Knowing in the end that your heart will be valued and cared for by you, whether or not you are confident the other person knows how to handle it with care, can provide the safety needed to risk allowing them in and giving it a try. In the moments they handle your heart well you can enjoy knowing and being known; you experience intimacy. In moments they don't, you know what to do and how to do it:"Above all else, guard your heart." When we communicate our needs, hurts, fears, dreams, goals, opinions, and beliefs with one another, meaningful communication can take place, and intimacy becomes possible.

"IN-TO-ME-SEE"=INTIMACY

**Reconciliation Tool 8A
"Identify Your Fears"**

Like the fears of emotional pain, rejection, and abandonment (which plague many of us in our human relationships), there are also other fears that are common when we think of being vulnerable with others. Below is a list of the most common fears that couples have expressed. Thinking of your own marriage relationship, number each reason with "1" (no fear), "2" (a little fear), "3" (a lot of fear). God wants you to cast your anxieties on Him and learn to trust Him to show you how to turn to Him with your fears. He will lead you out of the fear with confidence. (See *I Peter 5:7*).

_____ Fear of marriage ending.

_____ Fear of someone controlling you.

_____ Fear of being criticized/looking foolish.

_____ Fear of telling your spouse what your sexual wants are.

_____ Fear of discussing money issues (spending less or wanting more, etc.).

_____ Fear of financial security (retirement years, death of spouse, etc.)

_____ Fear of admitting mistakes and accidents (emotional or tangible).

WHERE'S YOUR HEART?: WEEK EIGHT — SECRET FEARS

_____ Fear of discussing the needs of your children.

_____ Fear of parenting issues (too strict/too lenient).

_____ Fear of discussing spiritual matters or opinions.

_____ Fear of rejection (jealousy, insecurities, etc.)

_____ Fear of sharing dreams and goals for the future (even if the dreams are some-times unrealistic).

_____ Fear of spouse's reaction of frustration/irritation.

_____ Fear of substance abuse (either yourself or spouse).*

_____ Fear of spouse's rage/anger /violence.*

_____ Fear of physical abuse.*

_____ Fear of children's safety (either physical or emotional).*

_____ Fear of suicide (either you or your spouse).*

_____ Other, not listed. _____

Reconciliation Tool 8B
"Identify Dangerous Situations"

While many of our fears involve emotional pain which is not life-threatening, some are founded on real-life dangers that need to be confronted. Developing a secure confidence in yourself and in your relationships will require both knowing how to accurately identify and acknowledge your fears, and then becoming skilled in handling them. If you numbered a "2" or "3" in any of the reasons which are marked with "*", it is important that you prepare to bring this fear to the light and confront the situation at hand. The emotion of fear often paralyzes people and stops them from taking the steps necessary to protect themselves and/or their children. The other extreme is when fear causes them to withdraw completely from the relationship. In both cases all people involved, as well as the relationship itself, are in some way compromised.

WHERE'S YOUR HEART?: WEEK EIGHT — SECRET FEARS

In the case of illegal behavior and/or physical or sexual abuse, it is important to contact your local authorities and report it immediately. If mental illness or deep psychological issues are present, consult your family physician for help and a referral. Otherwise:

1. **Contact an agency or support group in your area that deals with the crisis issues you are facing (most are listed in the front of your telephone directory).**

2. **If your situation allows it (time of day, day of week, and relationship with pastor) make an appointment with your pastor to discuss the crisis at hand and what the agency or support group has advised you to do.** We believe that it is important to include your church's advice along with the agency's advice. There is wisdom in more than one counselor in these situations, and because lives are in possible danger, it will be important that you get more than one person's advice.

3. **The most important thing for you to do in this situation is PRAY. Contact all of your support systems and ask for prayer—serious prayer.** If any one of them offers to fast and pray for you, take them up on their offer. You will need supernatural strength in order to get through this difficult time.

4. **Last, do not let your fear stop you from doing what you need to do.** If your marriage has any hope at all, it will be because you have not allowed fear to control your response to your spouse's behavior.

Reconciliation Tool 8C
"When Afraid, Rely on God"

In any situation that causes you to be afraid, even those that seem highly dangerous, God promises us that He will supply wisdom if we ask (see *James 1:5*). He will give us the supernatural strength through the Holy Spirit to face our fears, and He provides us words to speak (see *Luke 12:11*). And as with any skill- such as continued practice at turning to God in times of fear, receiving His supernatural strength, or speaking timely words of wisdom- you will get better and better the more you do it. After looking up the two following verses, rewrite them and personalize them as if the Lord wrote them to you. It will take practice to learn to be vulnerable with loved ones. Don't get discouraged if you feel fearful as you begin to speak up in truth.

1. *James 1:5* personalized:

WHERE'S YOUR HEART?: WEEK EIGHT — SECRET FEARS

2. *Luke 12:11* personalized:

From Joe: *Some of the men I have counseled have been in some pretty volatile situations with their wives, and the fear of arguments escalating into physical violence has kept some of them from being truthful. I try to get them to realize that if they are ever going to have a great marriage, they need to begin telling the truth about everything-regardless of the reaction from their spouse, and that no matter what, they need to work on being a godly husband. I caution them to use wisdom if they are going to discuss issues that typically cause their spouse to overreact, and to physically remove themselves if the situation escalates. I know from watching the guys who have done it (as well as myself), that as soon as they learn to fear God more than their wives, their marriage will just continue to improve. The key is to remember that it takes time-and some learn quicker than others. It took me three failed marriages and almost a fourth!*

From Michelle: *When I talk to women who fear being who they really are with their mate, it's usually rooted in their growing up years with a controlling parent. Many of the women (including myself) had a parent with a rage problem, and walking on eggshells in order to keep that parent from blowing up over some trivial matter was a way of life. The sad thing is that women (or men for that matter) will project what they think their spouse's reactions will be, based on how their raging parent reacted, and they will often create monsters that don't even exist. I know now that I did that with Joe many times. When we began to discuss our fears several years ago, I was amazed at how often I had misjudged what I thought his response would have been. Even on the issues that did make him angry, when I chose to be honest anyway, I realized that his response that I had imagined was always worse than the one he actually displayed. The best part about learning how to work through the fear of others' reactions is that it's a win-win situation. I remind the women I counsel that they (myself included) need to remember that we have a responsibility to God to be examples to the unbeliever, as well as to the believer, and everyone benefits as we overcome fear and our communication skills improve.*

WEEK EIGHT DISCUSSION QUESTIONS

Read the following questions and write in your answers in order to discuss them with your support partner during your weekly meeting time:

 Open in prayer

1. Look at what you wrote on tools 8A and 8B. Share with your support person any of the #2's or #3's that you feel comfortable discussing. (If you checked any questions marked with *, make certain you let them know if you have contacted your pastor or anyone else for help or referral. Please do not ask them to keep information like that to themselves and not involve outside help. It puts them in an unfair and compromising situation.)

2. Was there an opportunity this week to be vulnerable with your mate in an area that has normally been difficult? How about with someone else?

3. Is there anyone in your life at this time (besides possibly your spouse) whose reactions you fear? If so, how do you intend to begin changing the way you respond to their negative behavior? (Discuss the Scriptures you personalized.)

4. What did you relate to in Proverbs this week?

5. Share any additional thoughts, insights from the Lord, or experiences that have happened this week that challenged your thinking or impacted your heart.

6. What praise report and prayer concern do you have for this week?

 Close in prayer.

NOTES

WHERE'S YOUR HOPE?
*It is not **you** who is able to reconcile, by **Christ is you!***

"...for it is God who works in you to will and to act according to His good purpose"(Philippians 2:13).

WEEK NINE

Know How To Recognize Hope
But habits are hard to break.

We talk with many couples who admit that they can be doing just fine until something happens that causes one or both of them to react in the same old negative behavior pattern. Consequently, a chain reaction begins with one action triggering another. This often leads to "throwing in the towel;" or at least feeling like it. The couples who struggle the most with this roller-coaster-type behavior are couples who both have a problem being reactive rather than proactive. The term proactive was popularized in Stephen Covey's book, *7 Habits of Highly Effective People*. In essence this term means to "act before a situation becomes a crisis or a source of confrontation". Being reactive is a knee-jerk, "after the fact" behavior which creates the feeling of being "controlled" by life. In marriage, a proactive approach becomes pivotal to marital reconciliation.

Knowing what circumstances typically trigger the chain reaction and then having a plan on how to address the triggers will thwart the inevitable feelings of resignation. When one or both spouses have enough self-control and discipline to stop contributing to the cycle, the relationship will feel safer*. As described in the scenario below, there is more than one response to feeling frustrated. Joe found an alternative means of handling a frustrating circumstance. It can be difficult to come up with other alternatives, but if your marriage is to survive (not to mention other important relationships) it will be necessary to take the steps to start living life so that you are not always impatiently reacting to life's irritations and those around you.

* For an expanded understanding of this cycle and how to stop it, see Smalley and Paul's *ONA of Relationships* or *ONA of Relationships for Couples*.

From Joe: *One of the toughest things for me is to be able to say what I would like to say when I'm frustrated, in a way that doesn't come across harsh or loud. Michelle would sometimes say, "Stop yelling," when I didn't even realize that I was. I'm not that good with saying what I mean when we are arguing about something; she's much better with words than I am, so my frustration about that would just get me more worked up. My habit was to just walk out the door to get away from having to deal with whatever the issue was, but it was a habit that I wanted to change. So now, when I feel myself getting to that point, instead of leaving, I tell Michelle that I don't want to talk about the issue anymore at that time. She has learned that if she can give me some cooling off time, the situation at hand will get dealt with a lot sooner and better than if she continues to push to get it settled right then and there.*

From Michelle: *One time I heard a Christian speaker on the radio say that he could make major positive changes in a marriage if the mate with the most self-control and discipline was the only one that came in for counseling. His reasoning was that so much of our arguing and bad communication skills are reactive rather than proactive. I liked that concept, because I knew that if I could just have self-control, no matter what anyone else was doing, I would see some positive changes. I decided a long time ago that I would (as often as possible) practice self-control in frustrating situations in order to lessen the possibility of both of us overreacting*

WHERE'S YOUR HOPE?: WEEK NINE — KNOW HOW TO RECOGNIZE HOPE

at the same time. I must admit that it is still hard for me to be quiet when I want to continue on an issue until it is resolved.

But as Joe said, if I am patient and let him cool off and get his thoughts together, the situation turns out much better.

It would be unfair to lead you to believe that we never fall into some of our old behavior patterns now and then. But it is true that we NEVER use the words divorce or separation, and we used to use them every time we argued. And, although we still disagree on issues from time to time, our wars (silent or otherwise) are almost extinct. They used to happen quite regularly.

Some couples just argue more than others, but the good news is that even when you "blow it" and behave in the ways that usually escalate into serious situations, one of you can always put into practice the new behavior and change the course of events. Remember that it will take both of you to completely stop the argument, but only one of you to practice enough self-control to create a cooling
off atmosphere.

> **Important:** This is not about walking on eggshells to keep peace; it's about being adult enough, godly enough, and self-disciplined enough to model the Christ-like behavior that is needed in stressful situations. Speaking truthfully and following God more than man is what applies here.

Remember that no matter what circumstance you are in, if you know Christ as your Savior, **nothing** is hopeless (see *Mark 10:27*). No matter what the old patterns of behavior have been, with the supernatural strength of Christ in you, you will be able to allow God to change you and mold you into the person He so desires you to be.

Reconciliation Tool 9A
"Recognize Where Your Hope Is"

For the past several weeks you have been reading through Proverbs, praying, spending time with other Christians, and learning to focus on God instead of problems with your spouse. If you haven't been doing all of the above, then you are missing an opportunity to know the hope that is within you through Christ Jesus. If there is any portion of the previous exercises that you have missed, go back and look at them now, and make an honest effort to implement them into your life for the remainder of your time in the workbook.

Below are statements that focus on important principles of God's promises in the Bible. Fill in the blanks and meditate on the verses as you think of how much God loves you, and how

WHERE'S YOUR HOPE?: WEEK NINE— KNOW HOW TO RECOGNIZE HOPE

much He desires to give you everything you need in order to be godly in the stressful situations of life. You will need these verses in your heart as you prepare for the next exercise and the last segment of the workbook. (These verses are taken from NIV Life Application Bible, and the verses in your Bible may read a little differently, so adjust the sentences accordingly.)

1. Romans 15:5-7: "May the God who gives _____ and _____ give you a spirit of _____ among yourselves as you _____ Christ Jesus, so that with one _____ and _____ you may glorify the God and Father of our Lord Jesus Christ. _____ one another, then, just as Christ _____ you, in order to bring _____ to _____."

2. Romans 8:8-9: "Those controlled by the _____ _____ cannot please God. You, however, are controlled not by the _____ _____ but by the _____, if the _____ of God _____ in you. And if anyone does not have the _____ of Christ, he does not _____ to Christ."

3. 1 Peter 1:13-16: "Therefore, prepare your _____ for _____; be _____ _____; set your _____ fully on the grace to be given you when Jesus Christ is revealed. As _____ children, do not _____ to the evil desires you had when you lived in ignorance. But just as He who called you is _____, so be _____ in all you do; for it is _____: "Be _____, because I _____ _____."

From Joe: *I like to remind the guys that it's not about being "macho" in our homes, it's about being men of God. Most of the guys I know come into marriage not knowing how to be godly husbands and fathers because they came from homes where it wasn't being taught to them. I get real excited when I think about how we are able to change the course of events in our families and generations to come just by taking these principles from God's Word, and applying them to our lives now. It's never hopeless where God's concerned...in fact, the more hopeless it looks, the more excited I get...because I know from experience that nothing is too big for God!!!*

From Michelle: *Most women get concerned about the issues in their marriage long before the husband does. The problem is that many of them give up instead of going to serious prayer and being godly women in the midst of their circumstances. That's what this workbook is all about; staying focused on God and what He is able to accomplish when things appear hopeless! Yes, bad habits are hard to break, but like Joe tells the guys, nothing is too big for God. The question is, will we wait believing and trusting, or will we take matters into our own hands and miss the blessing He has for us?*

WHERE'S YOUR HOPE?: WEEK NINE — KNOW HOW TO RECOGNIZE HOPE

THE MUSCLE WE NEED TO EXERCISE MOST IS NOT OF A PHYSICAL NATURE, IT IS OF A SPIRITUAL NATURE....IT'S OUR FAITH MUSCLE.

So Jesus said to them, "...if you have faith as small as a mustard seed, you can say to this mountain, 'Move from here to there,' and it will move. Nothing will be impossible for you" (Matthew 17:20).

Reconciliation Tool 9B
"Practice Being Proactive"

It takes practice to learn to be proactive. One of the best ways to become disciplined and learn self- control is to identify what situations are more likely to lead to an emotional trigger; those that normally cause you to be reactive rather than proactive. Next, identify your typical response and then come up with two alternative responses. Last, allow yourself to be put in a specific situation in which you would typically react. By choosing to be in the situation, you've already exercised a measure of personal power and self-control. When you choose to respond, rather than just react, personal power and self-control are reinforced. In the future, when similar situations arise, you will be better prepared. Below are some suggestions or you can create a list of your own. Remember that it is Christ who will give you the patience, strength, and capacity to be godly if you will put your trust in Him and obey.

1. **Go to a store or restaurant that you know has rude or incompetent help, or wait for an opportunity to come along (you probably won't have to wait too long!) and determine that you are going to remain adult, courteous, and godly in your interactions no matter how annoying the situation is.** If possible, use the clerk or waiter/ waitress's name and give a genuine compliment before leaving. (If you try hard enough you can always find something nice to say to someone.)

2. **If you tend to be impatient, look for opportunities this week to wait without complaining, grumbling under your breath or reminding others you are still there.** Example: long grocery lines (choose to get in a long one), slow signal lights, bad drivers, procrastinating bosses/employees/ children/spouse, etc.

3. **Decide that the next time someone in your home has control of the TV remote, you will quietly let them channel-surf and no matter what, you will be pleasant through the half sentences and mixed plots, despite never seeing the end of the shows.**

4. **Call a friend or relative who has a tendency to get on your nerves because of negative remarks or endless chatter, and spend some time with them being genuinely interested in what they have to say.** Determine that you will actually listen and not tune out

WHERE'S YOUR HOPE?: WEEK NINE— KNOW HOW TO RECOGNIZE HOPE

one word. If you meet in person, make eye contact and remark on what they've said without giving criticism or correction.

5. **If you've never volunteered for child care at your church, do it this week, and decide beforehand that you will pay attention to each child's need and conversation.**

6. **Ask your spouse (if possible) or someone who loves and knows you well, such as a child, sibling, or parent, to tell you a couple areas in which you may need to improve.** Decide before you ask that no matter what they say, you will make eye contact, not get defensive, and listen. By the way, be prepared for them to wonder what you're up to! It's fun to watch the responses, but be prayed up for this, and make it a point to take the criticism for the purpose of learning self-control and character growth.

Choosing to be proactive in your dealings with others not only helps you, but it helps the other person as well. You can see by the above situations that in all of them there is the possibility for growth and encouragement for everyone involved. A couple of examples of how we have learned to be proactive are:

From Joe: *I know that when I get together with Michelle's large family they will talk and talk about all the things everyone used to do, and they relive and retell a lot of the same stories. I used to feel left out, but now I go to those get-togethers, prepared, knowing that's just how it's going to be. Instead of focusing on feeling left out, I decide before we even get there to listen (or try to, since they all like to talk at the same time!), and I take pictures and help create new memories.*

From Michelle: *When we go out of town for any longer than a day, it's a big deal. We have to make arrangements for our animals, our business, our son and granddaughter if they're not going with us (and if they are, that's a preparation all in itself), get the cars in order, get the house cleaned, pack, and f-i-n-a-l-l-y...leave for our fun, restful, vacation (?). Well, by the time we are ready to leave we're exhausted and irritable...and usually hungry. I used to get upset because it was always such a disappointment to be leaving for vacation irritated with one another, not to mention how stressful Joe would get when 5 minutes from home one of us would say, "When are we going to eat?" So, now, I just know that's how it's going to be, and we eat a snack before leaving. About 30 minutes down the road when we're relaxed and on our way, we begin to enjoy the trip!*

Some situations can be changed or negotiated, and others are just going to remain the same. No matter how frustrated you become, remember that God is at your side. He knew that you would be facing these challenges before they happened. He will take the trials you go through and use them to help you to grow spiritually, and learn how to better rely on Him.

"Jesus said, 'In the world ye shall have tribulation,' i.e., everthing that is not spiritual makes for my undoing, but--'Be of good cheer, I have overcome the world.' I have to learn to score off the things that come against me, and in that way produce the balance of holiness; then it becomes a delight to meet opposition." **Oswald Chambers, My Utmost for His Highest, December 4.**

WHERE'S YOUR HOPE?: WEEK NINE — KNOW HOW TO RECOGNIZE HOPE

Recognize Hope and Change Bad Habits By:

~ See stressful situations as opportunities to practice self-control.

~ Learn to be proactive rather than reactive.

~ Take a few minutes to pray when the circumstances would normally cause you to overreact, and then respond with your new tools.

~ Make a list of typically stressful situations and decide beforehand how you will change your behavior when the situation occurs.

~ Ask for forgiveness from God and the other person involved, when you "blow it" by reacting negatively in stressful situations.

~ Remember that when you give up a bad habit, make sure to replace it with a good one. When you pull up weeds, if you don't plant something in their place, the weeds will return.

WEEK NINE DISCUSSION QUESTIONS

Read the following questions and write in your answers in order to discuss them with your support partner during your weekly meeting time:

 Open in prayer

1. When you and your spouse disagree on something, what is a typical argument like? Are you silent, talkative, pouty, shouty, etc.?

2. What habits do you have that you wish you didn't? Were you able to begin working on any of them this week? If not, why?

3. Do you tend to be reactive rather than proactive?

4. Did you have an opportunity to practice any of the situations this week that would help build your self-control? If so, share the experience. If not, do you plan to, and if so, which example?

5. Of the Scriptures that you looked up this week, which one spoke to you the most?

6. Were you able to ask a relative close to you (or your spouse) to share one area that you should work on? How did it go?

7. What proverb meant the most to you this week? (Also see Proverbs 17:27-28.)

8. Share any additional thoughts, insights from the Lord, or experiences that have happened this week that challenged your way of thinking or impacted your heart.

9. What is a praise that you have for the week? What is a prayer request?

 Close in prayer.

NOTES

WEEK TEN

Know What To Avoid

God's timing is not always ours.

As we pointed out in the previous lesson, bad habits are hard to break, but are relatively easy to create. In the face of stressful situations in marriage, like most areas in life, we typically react impulsively in an attempt to alleviate our discomfort as soon as possible. We don't usually pause and think, or pause and pray before we act; we just act. We repeat the same or similar behaviors over and over again until they become habits. Our reactions may not really work all that well for us, and often don't make anyone around us all that happy; we just don't know what else to do. In fact, in the midst of stress most of us not only don't know how to be in tune with God's will and timing in order to make wise decisions, we may not even know there is another way. We just want to feel better…now!

Like it or not, there are many situations that take time in order for real change to occur and for trust to be rebuilt. In severe crisis situations where separation or the involvement of a third party has occurred, it will be difficult to make wise decisions because of the level of emotional pain and frustration. But regardless of how difficult your situation is, you have a personal responsibility before the Lord to know what His Word says, and then to obey. In fact, unless we are wrong about how much our Father in heaven loves us (and we know we're not), following God will always be in our best interest. The following are some examples of typical statements that we hear from those whose marriages are facing a crisis and may be making decisions reactively, rather than taking the time necessary to approach the decisions patiently with the benefit of godly wisdom:

"I know my spouse has been living with another person for the past 6 months, but he/she called last night and said he/she loved me and the kids and wants to come home, so I'm letting him/her move home today...we can always get counseling later..."

"Our divorce is almost final, and there's no hope my spouse will want to reconcile, so why shouldn't I go into the
singles class at church and get on with my life by meeting someone new?"

"Yes, these are physical abuse marks, but my spouse is just frustrated right now and if I push him/her to go to counseling it isn't going to help matters…"

"I know that my spouse says he/she is sorry for the hurt and pain the affair caused, but I have biblical grounds for divorce and I just don't think God expects me to have to remain married to him/her…"

"Look, my spouse and I have been separated for 4 years now. Just how long am I supposed to wait…?"

From Joe: The first time Michelle and I reconciled, we both continued doing things that caused problems in our marriage. I was a new Christian, and didn't have an accountability

WHERE'S YOUR HOPE?: WEEK TEN — KNOW WHAT TO AVOID

group of guys like I do now, so I had no one to talk to when I became frustrated. By the time we separated again 8 months later, I had let things build up inside of me. During the second separation I joined a Bible study, and it helped a lot to have that support system in place when we reconciled again two years later. Now I participate in a men's group and know the importance of making sure I'm accountable and help others to do the same.

From Michelle: *Both of us made the mistake of believing that our desire alone was enough to reconcile the first time. Without a knowledge of God's Word, and how to live a godly life, and without a support system in place we were "sitting ducks" for Satan's attacks following our reconciliation. The second time we reconciled we knew what to avoid, and we practiced staying away from those behaviors.. We've learned through the years that those same principles still apply.*

Reconciliation Tool 10A
"Six Things to Avoid When Attempting to Follow God"

Based on our own experience and on those we have counseled over the years, we believe that what you don't do is sometimes just as important as what you do. In each of the six recommendations, look up the suggested Scripture at the end and write it out, personalizing it with your name.

Example: *Psalm 46:10, "(your name), Be still and know that I am God."*

(I) Avoid Being Overly Confident

Being confident that Christ can heal your marriage is good, but being confident that He will do it no matter what, just because you've asked, borders on pride and self-centeredness. God's Word warns us about boasting, and cautions us to be patient as He allows everyone involved to learn what needs to be learned. It is helpful to remember that there are other factors and other people's free will involved in our situations.

Another thing to avoid in the area of boasting is thinking that because you are a child of God you deserve to be happy and should never have to suffer. We live in a messed up, fallen world. God does ultimately want you to be happy, but realistically there are no guarantees in this life. Actually, God's Word says that suffering is likely in verses such as Philippians 1:29, "For it has been granted to you on behalf of Christ not only to believe on Him, but also to suffer for Him." But honestly, in this life some suffering is likely for all of us.

Write out and personalize *Proverbs 27:1*:

WHERE'S YOUR HOPE?: WEEK TEN — KNOW WHAT TO AVOID

(2) Avoid Making Hasty Decisions

If you are ever in a situation in your marriage where you feel backed into a corner or forced to make a quick decision and you are confused, God's counsel in His Word is to wait (such as in *Psalm 46:10* quoted earlier). We have watched many couples make quick, irrational decisions, because they felt pressured by others and were tired of feeling confused. God does not work that way. Waiting on God, and knowing that He will guide your every step if you let Him is a hard concept for many to grasp, but that's exactly what He wants you to learn. God wants to equip you through His Word, other believers, and the Holy Spirit. He wants you to be able to make decisions with the quiet confidence of knowing that as long as you seek to do His will, He will ultimately work out everything in your best interest, as Romans 8:28 promises.

Write out and personalize *1 Corinthians 14:33* and *Philippians 4:5-7*:

(3) Avoid Too Many Counselors

God tells us throughout the Book of Proverbs that there is wisdom in receiving counsel from others, but He also warns us that balance and restraint of our tongue will help us to avoid foolishness. Oftentimes when there are problems in marriage one or both parties get into the habit of asking others what to do. If you've ever found yourself in that situation, you've probably also experienced the problem that can occur when too many people get involved; everyone has a different answer to your problem. We have found that it is best to keep your "advice circle" to about 3 or 4 people who themselves seek godly counsel and are not emotionally involved in your life. Parents and close friends will tend to give you advice to make you happy, and knowing details about your marital problems can also cause them to harbor negative feelings toward your spouse.

Another reason for avoiding too many counselors is that God wants you to depend on Him to meet your deepest needs through prayer and knowledge of His Word, instead of running to everyone else when you have a problem. Unfortunately, many people never learn how to hear from God directly or develop the ability to become personally discerning. They instead make decisions primarily based on the advice of those they trust, without taking the important final step of personal communication with God. Without the valuable skill of discernment, your well-being is only as good as the wisdom of your counselors. As wise and well intended as they may be, they are still human.

Write out and personalize *Psalm 116:1-3* and *Matthew 11:29-30*:

WHERE'S YOUR HOPE?: WEEK TEN — KNOW WHAT TO AVOID

(4) Avoid Rescuing and "Playing God"

Many well-meaning Christians have a difficult time letting people suffer their own consequences of sin or foolishness, and that can especially include our own spouse or children. This is an important principle to learn because if you continue to get in the way of God's lessons for those you love (or allow others to get in the way of your lessons) it will take much longer and be more painful in the end. There are many examples of God's people getting in the way of His timing or discipline of others. Even though God's plan is never thwarted by men, in all of those examples mentioned in the Bible, people suffered in ways that were often unnecessary. Moses spent 40 years in the desert after he tried to "help" his people in his own timing, rather than waiting for God's timing (*Exodus 2:11-15*).And Rebekah never again saw her favored son, Jacob, after she deceitfully "helped" him receive his father's blessing (*Genesis 27:41-45*).

If your spouse behaves in a way that is causing some painful consequences in his or her life (for instance; from their job, church, the law, or friends), love them, encourage them, and pray for them, but don't try to fix the situation and rescue them from their learning experience. It will only result in resentment because you will be acting as a "parent figure" instead of their "helpmate," as God intended. Additionally, they're less likely to learn what they need to learn. And to top it off, you will also risk losing a measure of respect for your spouse. Typically, the unconscious result of rescuing someone from their problems is forever after seeing them as unable to get out of their own "mess" without your help.

Write out and personalize *Proverbs 19:19* and *Hebrews 12:11*:

(5) Avoid Being Paralyzed By Fear

Remember when we gave you the principle of fear, and encouraged you to rely on God when you're afraid? If you haven't been practicing it, start now. Fear is the opposite of faith, and as a Christian it is critical to learn how to trust God. No one is more interested in your ultimate success and well-being then He is. Many couples never reconcile simply because they fear the risk of being hurt again, embarrassed again, or disappointed again. Once you've understood what God wants you to do, don't wait – do it. Obedience is crucial once God opens the door and shows you His timing has come. When God's word seems to contradict your feelings, always opt for obeying God's word. Your feelings do matter, and it's sometimes hard to trust God when we are feeling fear. Pay attention to what you are feeling, but attend to those feelings in a godly way by letting your Father in heaven lead you. If you want to experience peace and joy, obey God, and step out in faith.

WHERE'S YOUR HOPE?: WEEK TEN — KNOW WHAT TO AVOID

When the Williams reconciled, no one in their family thought they should. Everyone thought they were making a mistake (including a few Christian counselors they had talked with who counseled them to wait longer). But through seeking God's will on their own, and with an absolute certainty that God had moved in both of their lives, they took their step of faith. They both believed that in their desire to obey God, if their timing had been off, He would have stopped them. They know from *Acts 16:7* that God halted Paul and his companions, *"...they tried to enter Bithynia, but the Spirit of Jesus (or Holy Spirit) would not allow them to."*

"The paralysis of refusing to act (when God reveals a truth) leaves a man exactly where he was before; when once he acts, he is never the same." Oswald Chambers, *My Utmost for His Highest*, November 4.

Write out and personalize *2 Timothy 1:7* and *Matthew 10:26-27*:

(6) Avoid Comparing Your Marriage with Others

This seems like a pretty obvious statement, but it's often more difficult to avoid than we realize. God is quite clear on His message to us regarding coveting other people's possessions (including their husband or wife), but the issue of desiring a "great marriage" can also turn into coveting, resulting in sin.

From Michelle: *Several years ago, Joe and I were showing some Gary Smalley videos on marriage in our class. It had been about the sixth time we'd seen them, and I found myself feeling a little resentful towards Joe because he wasn't saying and doing some of the things to me that Gary Smalley did for his wife! "After all," I thought, "hasn't he seen these videos enough to know exactly how to talk and behave like Gary says?" Little by little, over the next couple of weeks, my resentment grew as I focused on things in our marriage that I thought could be so much better and more like my imagined "perfect-Smalley-marriage." Not long after, my discontentment began to show in little negative comments, as I began to wonder what it would be like to have the kind of marriage the Smalleys had. One day, Joe in his frustration of trying to figure out what was going on with me, asked, and I told him. In his amazement that I had told him I was angry because he wasn't more like Gary Smalley, he confidently looked me square in the eyes and quipped;"Michelle, if I were more like Gary Smalley, I'd be traveling all over the countryside doing seminars and I'd never be home!" That brought me back to reality, and I realistically and thankfully let Joe know how much I appreciated his being home with me.*

The above story is an example of how quickly a person can set unrealistic marital goals by becoming focused on wanting what you imagine someone else has, including their marriage. One of the worst things you can do is to compare your spouse to another person. It borders on

WHERE'S YOUR HOPE?: WEEK TEN — KNOW WHAT TO AVOID

lusting for someone else and can cause deep emotional pain. This is especially the case when a spouse is sensitive and has low self- esteem because of past hurts. Plus, all of us bring our own set of challenges into our relationships, and the person you are comparing your spouse to is no exception – even Gary Smalley!

While comparing your marriage to someone else's may not be as personal, it can still cause pain and frustration because you are putting expectations on you and your spouse that you may not be able to live up to. Each person was purposely and intentionally created by God, and as a result every marriage has its own personality and profile. It is based on your temperaments as well as who God has purposed you to be in your particular family unit. Set goals to have a great marriage, but let God design it His way, and let it be unique. No two marriages are the same...but they can all uniquely glorify God because He designed marriage as an example of Christ and the Church (see *Ephesians 5:31-32*).

Write out and personalize *Romans 12:3-5* and *Galatians 5:24-26*:

God's timing is never the same for everyone, even though the situations they are in might be similar. The six principles we have shared with you are to help you stay focused on God so that whatever crisis or circumstance you face, you will be able to relax in the knowledge that God is right there by your side. Trust Him, and ask Him to give you wisdom, and He always will. He promises in *James 1:5, "If any of you lacks wisdom, he should ask God, who gives generously to all without finding fault, and it will be given to him."*

WEEK TEN DISCUSSION QUESTIONS

Read the following questions and write in your answers in order to discuss them with your support partner during your weekly meeting time:

 Open in prayer

1. Do you tend to have a hard time knowing if it is your will or God's will when you make a decision?

2. If you answered yes, what are some of the ways that you have made decisions in the past and God confirmed that they were His will?

3. Can you remember a time that you tried to do something on your own and God stopped you?

4. In your study of Scriptures this week, which ones were especially helpful?

5. Of the six principles we shared, which one related to you the most?

6. Which proverb spoke to you this week in your regular reading?

7. Share any additional thoughts, insights from the Lord, or experiences that have happened this week that challenged your thinking or impacted your heart.

8. What is a praise you have, and what is a prayer request for this week?

 Close in prayer.

NOTES

WEEK ELEVEN

Know Who Is On Your Team
Turn opposition into optimism.

Have you ever wondered why we have to have so much opposition in life? The answer: *because we are born.*

So, how are we supposed to be able to turn all of the opposition we face into optimism? The answer: *if we have accepted Jesus as our Lord and Savior, we are "born again."* God tells us in His Word that if we are to enter into the kingdom of God we must be born again of the spirit (*John 3:5-7*). Once we have the spirit of God in us, we will be able to understand the things of God through His Spirit (*John 14:25-26*).

Our pastor (Joe and Michelle's) recently pointed out that we are plagued with eternal enemies: anxieties, envy, jealousy, bitterness, lust, and (everyone's favorite) worry. He concluded his sermon by pointing us to God and His promises of peace, direction and wisdom. "All you have to do," he encouraged, "is surrender your life to God, draw near to Him, and claim and believe His promises." That part's easy. But it takes action, dedication, and obedience on our part. That part is harder, but the benefits can be amazing. Turn opposition in your marriage into optimism so you can experience God's peace.

When trials and opposition come into your marriage, two main options are available: (1) make decisions on your own and do things your way, or (2) work *with* God and do things His way. Your way (apart from God) is a set-up for frustration and disappointment. It cheats you out of the opportunity to be led by our God, the creator and sustainer of the universe. He is the one who knows how things are supposed to work, and always has our best interests in mind. Collaborating with God and doing things His way allows Him to work *through* you, so that His perfect will is accomplished by way of the opposition.

The most likely outcome from battling opposition on your own is that you will come away feeling discouraged, worried, and hopeless. However, following God in the face of opposition will at the very least build character, and will shine the light of Christ through you – potentially causing others to want to know Him because of you. But best of all, don't forget that God is for you and wants you to have an awesome marriage. Given half a chance He will work through the opposition with you to create a stronger marriage (which ultimately glorifies God).

Reconciliation Tool 11A
"Rate Your Oppositions"

Below is a list of common oppositions that most marriages face. Rate each one with a "**1**" *not very often*, "**2**" *sometimes*, and "**3**" *frequently*. In some cases you may not identify with very many at all. However, if you are separated from your spouse, or if you have recently reconciled, you may identify with all of the oppositions listed. Don't be discouraged. We have

WHERE'S YOUR HOPE?: WEEK ELEVEN — KNOW WHO IS ON YOUR TEAM

witnessed (as the Williams experienced in their own reconciliation) the most exciting opportunities for glorifying God and personal growth that would have never been possible otherwise. These choices are based on outside oppositions that come against your marriage.

Rate the Opposition:

____ In-law problems (either parents).

____ Step-children conflicts (either you or your spouse).

____ Out of work (either of you).

____ Financial problems.

____ Opposition from friends or family concerning the reconciliation of your marriage (either toward you, your spouse, or both of you).

____ A third party involved (with you or your spouse).

____ Some type of injustice directed at you or your spouse.

____ A loss (either financial or a death in family).

____ Illness or physical problems (either you or your spouse).

____ Problems with children (biological).

____ Misunderstanding or conflict with other believers/church.

____ Problems with authorities (government or law, either of you).

____ **Total**

If your totals are above 20 you are under quite a bit of stress trying to deal with all of the opposition in your life. Remember, this week's lesson is about opposition that comes against your marriage--not opposition from you or your spouse against one another. It is important that you understand what we want to show you here. All marriages have outside opposition that tries to divide it because a healthy marriage represents Christ and the Church, and as a result Satan opposes the institution of marriage; he is the true enemy of your marriage.

WHERE'S YOUR HOPE?: WEEK ELEVEN — KNOW WHO IS ON YOUR TEAM

Few things can more effectively destroy you, your marriage, and the witness of the church than when a husband and wife mistakenly see each other as the enemy. Whether you realize it or not your spouse is not the enemy, but is your teammate in a common cause. Once a husband and wife begin to understand this truth they can begin working on turning that opposition into optimism. When a couple faces opposition from outside factors such as the ones mentioned above, it can cause the couple to join forces and come against the problem together, creating a united front.

While on a missionary trip to another country, one pastor noticed that the family units of that culture were unusually strong and that there was a keen sense of unity among the people. Because of the severe conditions they lived in, they needed each other in order to keep outside opposition from destroying them physically. The simple revelation was that they were united against a common "enemy." In the face of adversity they pulled together rather than pulled apart. "A house divided against itself will fall" (*Luke 11:17*). But working together with God we can do amazing things.

> **When couples mistakenly view each other as the enemy, they are weakening their forces to fight the real enemy: Satan.**

When couples mistakenly view each other as the enemy, they are weakening their forces to fight the real enemy: Satan.

God warns us in the Bible that we are in a spiritual battle, and the enemy wants to destroy marriages and families. The sad truth is that Satan appears to be winning as we see the rise of divorces within the church. But it isn't too late! You can join forces with your mate and reclaim lost ground for your family and future generations. Even with an unwilling spouse, you alone can change the tone of your relationship by beginning to approach your spouse as your teammate and not your enemy; even if they don't. You can also teach your children how to view opposition, and show them through your example how to fight against the attacks on the family.

From Joe: *When I heard that pastor tell the story about how those families in the foreign country were united against a common enemy, from that night on I viewed the problems Michelle and I faced in a whole new way. I realized that, as the head of the family, I had an obligation before God to stand for truth and righteousness and to equip my family with the right kind of protection: spiritual protection. When Michelle and I started seeing each other as united against an outside enemy that wanted our marriage destroyed, it changed the way we viewed every bit of opposition that we faced from then on.*

From Michelle: *Joe and I realized that if we could stop Satan from destroying our marriage relationship, through the supernatural power God had equipped us with (His Holy Spirit), that we weren't just saving our marriage, but the marriages in future generations. It's a fact that people who come from divorce have a higher divorce rate, and we decided that we would stop*

WHERE'S YOUR HOPE?: WEEK ELEVEN — KNOW WHO IS ON YOUR TEAM

the cycle. I'm so thankful that Joe took the lead spiritually, but even if he hadn't, I knew that God was saying to me, "enough is enough" and that living my life my way and not following God was never going to be an option for me anymore.

Reconciliation Tool 11B
"Build Your Team"

Building the marriage team to fight the spiritual battle you are facing is much like building an army or any other team that depends on one another in order to stay alive. In order for your marriage to be healthy, you need to make certain that everyone who is on your team will bring strength and unity. We want to give you two important principles for building your team based on the truths of God's promises in His Word. Even if you are not living with your spouse, follow these principles. Your reconciliation and how you come out of this crisis will be greatly influenced by how well you learn to face opposition, with or without your mate.

(1) Identify Your Team

■ **The first thing you need to do is to make sure that the people who say they are rooting for your marriage know how to pray for your marriage.** Since you are in a spiritual battle, your team can extend beyond your marriage to include your support network of friends and family. They can join with you in fighting your common enemy. Since the best weapon your team can use is prayer, make certain that you build your team with committed Christians who believe in the power of Christ.

Second, take an inventory of how they have supported you so far. Have they followed through if you asked them to be supportive of you while you went through the workbook? Have they helped keep you accountable, and encouraged you to speak respectfully of your spouse even when you might have been frustrated with him/her? Finally, don't worry if your team is small. A few strong Christians praying for you and your spouse are more powerful than a lot of well-meaning friends and family who build an alliance with you against your spouse.

Write out and personalize *Matthew 26:41* and *Proverbs 15:29*:

(2) Join Forces with Your Spouse

If you are living with your spouse and he/she has agreed to participate in this workbook, then you are on your way to building a strong fortress. If not, this next step is going to require that you be stretched a bit, and you will need to have your extended team praying hard for you. It's important that you go to your mate and ask forgiveness, even if you have not been

WHERE'S YOUR HOPE?: WEEK ELEVEN — KNOW WHO IS ON YOUR TEAM

the only one in the wrong. As we bring you to the end of the workbook, you may need to take yet another step of faith at this point and obey God's Word in the area of love and marriage. In order to stand before God with any degree of integrity, you will need to continually humble yourself in order to allow the Holy Spirit to work in you and through you. Believe it or not, this actually becomes less painful over time as you begin to experience the Lord growing you in strength and character.

With a humble spirit, go to your spouse and say;"Will you forgive me for not being the husband/wife you have needed me to be? If the answer is yes, then ask if your spouse would consider allowing God to do a new work in your marriage, and consider reconciliation. If the answer is no, before you walk away calmly say, "If you change your mind, please let me know." Wait for God to work...don't give up! Your marriage is not over unless one of you dies or joins another partner.

Write out and personalize *Matthew 19:6* and *I Corinthians 13:4-7*:

**Reconciliation Tool 11C
"Seven Battle Strategies"**

For those of you standing on the battlefield with your mate at your side and your prayer team in place, the battle will of course be much easier than for those of you feeling alone because your mate is choosing not to participate at this time. But in either case you are not alone; God is at your side. Though this may be hard to imagine, for those of you standing alone with God, in some ways your battle may even be easier than those whose mates are with them. Paul said in *I Corinthians 7: 32-35*, those who are married have the cares of their spouse to be concerned with. So, the important thing is that as long as you can honestly say that you have tried to the best of your ability to walk with God toward reconciliation, God will equip you to fight the battle you are facing with the same strength He gives the husband and wife team. He will provide the power of the Holy Spirit to equip you.

> **With each outside opposition that comes, remember that it is an attack from the enemy to destroy your family and your marriage. Claim the victory through Christ.**

Read Paul's words to the Corinthians:

I would like you to be free from concern. An unmarried man is concerned about the Lord's affairs-how he can please the Lord. But a married man is concerned about the affairs of this world-how he can please his wife-and his interests are divided. An unmarried woman or virgin is concerned about the Lord's affairs: Her aim is to be devoted to the Lord in both body and

WHERE'S YOUR HOPE?: WEEK ELEVEN — KNOW WHO IS ON YOUR TEAM

spirit. But a married woman is concerned about the affairs of this world-how she can please her husband. I am saying this for your own good, not to restrict you, but that you may live in a right way in undivided devotion to the Lord (I Corinthians 7:32-35).

The 7 Battle Strategies to Implement when attacks come:

1. *Identify the source of the attack and ask God to give you love and understanding for all the people involved.*

    Write out and personalize *Matthew 5:44* (use a separate sheet of paper or back of page for the verses listed).

2. *Sometimes an attack will include emotional pain. Face the emotional pain rather than distracting oneself with behaviors that only lead to more pain (such as alcohol, drugs, lust, shopping, overeating, etc.).*

    Write out and personalize *1 Corinthians 6:9-10*.

3. *Get plenty of rest, eat right, exercise, and fellowship with your mate (if possible) and your support team during the attack.*

    Write out and personalize *1 Corinthians 6:19-20*, and *Ephesians 5:29*.

4. *If there is anything that you can do on your own behalf to be at peace and bring closure to the problem, do it. If it is out of your hands and you have done all you can, wait on God and pray.*

    Write out and personalize *Romans 12:18*.

5. *As you wait on God to act on your behalf, remember to offer up praise and thanks. This act is a demonstration of your faith as well as an act that will strengthen your faith (Acts 16: 22-40). Your praises are sweet to Him when you are in trouble and you must remember that Satan cannot do anything to you that God has not given permission for. God will never let you face more than you can handle.*

    Write out and personalize *1 Corinthians 10:13* and *Ephesians 5:19-20*.

6. *Remind your mate (if it's possible) that you love him/her, and that you know that God is in control of the situation. If you can hold one another, be intimate, or go for long walks together, do so. Spend as much time as you can just being an encouragement. Respect*

WHERE'S YOUR HOPE?: WEEK ELEVEN — KNOW WHO IS ON YOUR TEAM

your differences in the way you both respond to attacks. For instance, if one of you becomes irritable or negative when outside opposition happens, and the other more supportive or loving, learn to draw on those differences and come to a compromise before the attack happens in order to be proactive when difficulties come.

Write out and personalize *Ephesians 4: 15-16*:

7. Last, when the attack is over, if possible, celebrate with your mate by doing something you both enjoy. If you're alone, celebrate with God...a nice dinner, an overnight stay at the beach, etc. Thank God for bringing you through the battle, and if you went through the battle with your mate remind him/her that your marriage is now stronger because of the alliance you formed during the attack. Even if you went through the battle without the support of your mate, you'll be better equipped for the next time, and your character will have been strengthened. Much respect is gained when others watch us stand against opposition in a mature and godly manner.

Read *1 Peter 5:6-9*. Write out and personalize verse 10:

WHEN OPPOSITION COMES, GOD PROMISES TO GET US
THROUGH IT, NOT OUT OF IT

WEEK ELEVEN DISCUSSION QUESTIONS

Read the following questions and write in your answers in order to discuss them with your support partner during our weekly meeting time:

 Open in prayer

1. Discuss what God has been saying to you through your scripture reading this past week.

2. Name all the categories you checked on Tool IIA. How do those outside stressors affect your marriage?

3. Did you have an opportunity to ask your spouse for forgiveness, and to see if he/she would consider reconciliation? If so, how did it go?

4. Have you had an opportunity to use the 7 battle strategies yet? If so, how did it go? If not, how useful do you feel those will be to you? Why?

5. Have you typically perceived your spouse more as your ally or your enemy throughout marriage?

6. What were the high points in your life this past week?

7. What were the low points in your life this past week?

8. What do you need prayer for as you face this coming week?

 Close in prayer.

NOTES

WEEK TWELVE

Know When To "Go Forth"

Whatever the outcome, use it for good.

Many couples begin attending church in hopes of saving their troubled marriage. The sad truth is that statistics now show that the divorce rate is at least as high within the church as it is outside. Christian or non-Christian, marriage troubles are painful. It is even more painful to go through a divorce when one of you wants desperately to save the marriage.

It is our prayer that regardless of the outcome of your marriage relationship, you will understand what it means to reconcile God's way. If you have followed the workbook as we suggested, and have been learning to focus on God rather than your mate, your life will never be the same. God blesses those who desire to obey Him, and He will allow whatever circumstance you are now facing to glorify Him. For some of you, your marriage will be much stronger and you will never again use the words divorce or separation in your vocabulary with one another. Others of you might have been separated when you began the workbook, and may have even reconciled within the past three months. Possibly, some of you are seeing small changes, but realize that it will take time for complete healing to occur. And finally, there are those of you who will become a statistic because of your spouse's choices.

BE ENCOURAGED, WHATEVER CONDITION YOU ARE IN AT THE POINT,
KNOW THAT GOD NEVER WASTES PAIN!

"...the Father of compassion and the God of all comfort, who comforts us in all our troubles, so that we can comfort those in any trouble with the comfort we ourselves have received from God" (2 Corinthians 1:3-4).

From Joe: *I like to tell the guys (and I remember when I had to do this) that no matter what happens, whether our wife decides to stay in the marriage or not, that we have to be about the business of God and we have to obey God's Word. We are to be the light in a dark world (or home), wherever God has us, and the only way we can be light is if we act as conduits for God's electricity (love) to flow out of us. Michelle has often said that most women she talks to want a godly, loving husband more than any other thing, even more than financial security. And yet I know many guys that will use the excuse of work to not spend time learning about God in order to become men of God, and then wonder why their marriage is in trouble.*

From Michelle: *There were many times during the troubles in our marriage that I prayed for God to just get me out of it any way possible. I used to think being a godly widow sounded good (and I've heard others say the same). I just wanted the problems to go away. In looking back, I'm now so thankful that God didn't rescue me out of my situation. I have been able to comfort women in a way that I would not have been able to otherwise. Even though it was painful at the time, God has now been able to use that pain to help others get through theirs. I*

WHERE'S YOUR HOPE?: WEEK TWELVE — KNOW WHEN TO "GO FORTH"

always remind women that as long as they do things God's way, and stand blameless before Him (1 Corinthians 1:8), He will use every situation they encounter to glorify Him to others.

Reconciliation Tool 12A
"Prepare For the Journey"

Jesus' last command to His disciples before He departed to join His Father in heaven was the "Great Commission" (*Matthew 28:16-19*). He expected them (and us) to make disciples of all nations, and teach everyone about God's Word, and the importance of obeying everything He commanded. If you love God, you will want to obey Him, and you will want to give comfort to others just as He has comforted you. So, it will be important to begin to prepare for the direction of ministry God might call you to, when the time is right.

We have watched many people come through their marital crisis successfully because of their love for God and their obedience to Him. By successfully, we mean following God and feeling the Lord's peace and joy in spite of their circumstances--not necessarily that their marriage was saved. In every successful case, there was a desire to "go forth" for the Lord's work. We have listed a few of the ministries some of the people have gone into. Look over the list and mark the ones that might spark an interest for you, and begin praying about a direction to which the Lord might lead you.

____ Reconciliation ministry; helping others in relationship crisis.

____ Men's/Women's ministry; support groups or Bible studies.

____ Children's ministry; either children from separated and divorced homes or serving in child care setting for stressed dads or moms.

____ Freedom ministry; helping others overcome identity problems with Christ, and equipping believers for spiritual battle.

____ Addiction ministries; helping others in the areas of addiction or co-dependency.

____ Divorce recovery ministry; helping those who are divorced begin their life again.

The above examples are just a few of the areas we have seen God lead couples or single adults into after they have come through a marriage crisis and obeyed Him in the midst of their struggles. On the following pages are four suggestions that we recommend in order to be equipped for wherever God might lead you.

WHERE'S YOUR HOPE?: WEEK TWELVE — KNOW WHEN TO "GO FORTH"

Know your spiritual gifts

In God's Word He tells us that when we become believers we are all given spiritual gifts in order to use them within the Body of Christ. Most churches have their own test, or have access to tests referred to as the "spiritual gifts test." This test reveals what your natural abilities are concerning such things as: teaching, serving, administration, etc. The purpose of this test is not to put you in a "box" or tell you that you cannot serve in some other area. It is so you can serve to your fullest potential and avoid burnout. You can also go on-line and take an on-line test to assess your spiritual gifts. One suggestion is www.christianet.com/bible/spiritualgiftstest.htm

Read I Corinthians 12:7-11, and look through the list of different spiritual gifts. See if any seem to fit you, and pray about how God may want you to use your gifts.

Know God's Word

If you are not yet in a Bible study, make this a priority in your life. Studying God's Word is different from reading it in your quiet time. It requires homework, discipline and accountability that are necessary character qualities when you step out into ministry.

Read Proverbs 1:1-7 and list the reasons for studying God's Word.

Know when it's time

As we studied earlier, God's timing may not be the same as ours, and that's also true when volunteering for ministry. If you tend to procrastinate and feel unworthy of serving in a ministry, you may miss opportunities that God puts in your path. If you lean toward the other extreme, and tend to overextend yourself with goals and visions for "helping" God, you might end up burned-out, used up, and not be able to complete the "race" (*Acts 20:24, 2 Tim. 4:7*).

It's been our experience that when people experience a crisis in their marriage, the two extremes mentioned above seem to become exaggerated. People either avoid serving in ministry because of low self-respect and embarrassment, or they volunteer for everything and try to "help" others in order to transfer their own pain. Neither extreme is helpful to God in His plan to bring the Gospel to others. The first extreme keeps you focused on your own problems instead of helping others in need, and the second extreme gets you focused only on others, instead of getting and keeping your own home in order.

The church you belong to can help get you plugged-in to the ministry to which God is calling you. Each ministry or church will usually have requirements for serving, so there may be some

WHERE'S YOUR HOPE?: WEEK TWELVE — KNOW WHEN TO "GO FORTH"

lag time between your inquiry and opportunity to serve. In the meantime, here are three questions you can ask yourself to help you know God's timing for ministry involvement: (1) Do you love God and desire to have others love Him too? (2) Do you respect those in ministry leadership at your church, and are you willing to submit to their authority without grumbling? (3) Have you learned to prioritize your time so that your marriage and family won't suffer if you volunteer for service in a ministry at this time?

Read Isaiah 35:8 and 46:10-11, and list God's promises.

Reconciliation Tool 12B
"Trust God With The Outcome"

Only God sees the big picture, and only He knows the outcome of your marriage. Regardless of what you think would be best, God knows what is truly best for you. If you are His child, He will care for you like a loving parent cares for its young. All He asks you to do is trust Him, love Him, and obey His commands, and in return He promises to take care of everything else. Read the Scriptures below and write each one out and personalize it with your name. This will be in preparation for your last "Reconciliation Tool."

Isaiah 66:13:

Matthew 6:25-27:

Reconciliation Tool 12C
"Know The Way"

The last tool we want to give you is the most important tool you will use. It is Jesus, Himself. He is the One that will keep you focused, give you strength, and be by your side no matter what happens in your marriage, or any other area of your life. His love for you is greater than you could ever imagine. He is the Way to reconciling all of your relationships. Read the following Scripture verse and prepare to discuss with your support person how strong or weak your faith is these days.

WHERE'S YOUR HOPE?: WEEK TWELVE — KNOW WHEN TO "GO FORTH"

He is the image of the invisible God, the firstborn over all creation. For by Him all things were created: things in heaven and on earth, visible and invisible, whether thrones or powers or rulers or authorities; all things were created by Him and for Him. He is before all things, and in Him all things hold together. And He is the head of the body, the church; He is the beginning and the firstborn from among the dead, so that in everything He might have the supremacy. For God was pleased to have all His fullness dwell in Him, and through Him to reconcile to Himself all things, whether things on earth or things in heaven, by making peace through His blood, shed on the cross (Colossians 1:15-20).

Do you truly believe that Jesus loves you, and has come to heal the broken-hearted, and set the captives free? Do you believe that He wants you to have fullness in life? What would that look like, even in the midst of your current situation?

WHERE'S YOUR HOPE?: WEEK TWELVE — KNOW WHEN TO "GO FORTH"

What if you need more help?

Hopefully you now have a solid support system in place and will continue to stay connected. We all need good counsel from time to time. However, if you are still feeling that you need more, that is not uncommon, weird, or weak. You are going through challenges that none of us are really prepared or trained to handle alone. If you are seeing a good counselor or pastor that is both supporting and prompting you forward, both personally and relationally, stay connected with him/her. If you are not currently working with a good counselor or pastor, find one. If you don't know of one, ask your church for a referral, or call at the National Institute of Marriage (417) 335-5882 and we'll help you find one.

If you would like more information about the National Institute of Marriage Intensive Programs (our Marriage Emergency Room) call us at the above number or go to our website at www.nationalmarriage.com. Our website is filled with lots of useful information, books, articles, and plenty to help you decide if an Intensive is for you, or introduce you to a variety of other available resources. If you do call us our consultants will be happy to answer any questions you might have. But whatever you decide to do, if you are struggling don't try to go it alone. Stay connected to God, and allow yourself to be supported by your brothers and sisters in Christ – your spiritual family.

WEEK TWELVE DISCUSSION QUESTIONS

Please remember that it took longer than twelve weeks for your marriage to get into a crisis, so it may take longer than twelve weeks for you to realize full reconciliation in your marriage. The most important thing at this point is to stay focused on God and let Him continue to lead you into the plan He has for your life.

   Open in prayer

1) Go through the verses and questions from tool 12B and 12C, and discuss the ones that impacted you in some way.

2) Of these past 12 chapters, what three things have surprised you the most?

3) What have you learned about yourself?

4) What have you learned about your spouse?

5) How has this experience impacted your faith?

6) How are you different today from how you were when you started this program?

WEEK TWELVE DISCUSSION QUESTIONS

Now switch roles for a minute. Here are three questions for you to ask your support partner. (The person you are supporting will ask you these)

7) Ask your support partner how this experience has impacted him/her over the past twelve weeks.

8) Ask your support partner if he/she was surprised by any changes that happened over the twelve weeks.

9) Ask your support partner to give you feedback on what he/she sees as next steps for you.

■ Graciously thank your support partner for his/her investment in your life, and conclude in prayer together.

NOTES

IN CONCLUSION

As you step out in faith and trust God to be by your side during this time in your marriage, our prayers are with you. We have faith that God will bless your obedience and commitment to reconcile His way. Many of you will experience the miracle of a healed marriage that will bring joy to your life and glory to God, and we rejoice with you.

From Joe: *In conclusion, I'd like to leave the guys with some advice: Don't forget to keep protected with God's Armor (Ephesians 6:10). We're in a battle and you need to keep up the good fight. Stay in a men's group and always be accountable, love your wife...even if she doesn't return that love, and be about the business of God. And one last bit of advice: You've probably heard it said, "You stay out of my business and I'll stay out of yours." Well, God wants us to do the opposite: Get into His business, and He'll take care of ours. The verse I want to leave you with is one from Isaiah which says that as we walk in obedience He protects us from behind as well as in front:* **"Then your light will break forth like the dawn, and your healing will quickly appear; then your righteousness will go before you, and the glory of the Lord will be your rear guard" (Isaiah 58:8).**

From Michelle: *In closing I would like to say to the women: Pray for your husband when you are frustrated with him, instead of trying to change him or parent him. We have the opportunity as God's children to give Him our worries and cares, and then as we step out in obedience to Him, He will guide us through anything we face, including a troubled marriage. But we have to pray. It's hard sometimes because we are human and we all make mistakes, but God never makes mistakes, and we have to hold on to His promises. Use the workbook. If you are still in crisis, go back through it. Give your marriage time and give God time, and don't feel alone. God is with you and He loves you and He will guide your every step if you'll let Him. The verse I want to leave you with is from* **Isaiah 30:21, "Whether you turn to the right or to the left, your ears will hear a voice behind you, saying, 'This is the way; walk in it.'"**

Instead of leaving you with the words "The End," we want to remind you that it's just ...

The Beginning!

Marriage 911: First Response

Recommended Reading and Resource List

Anderson, Nancy C.
Avoiding the Greener Grass Syndrome: How to Grow Affair-Proof Hedges Around Your Marriage. Grand Rapids, MI: 2004.

Chapman, Gary D.
The Five Love Languages. Chicago: Northfield, 1992, 1995.

Chapman, Gary D.
Hope For The Separated. Chicago: Moody, 1982, 1996.

Chambers, Oswald.
My Utmost For His Highest. England: Oswald Chambers Publications Assn., Ltd., renewed 1963. 1986.

Shriver. Gary and Mona
Unfaithful: Rebuilding Trust After Infidelity. Cook Communications: 2005.

Thomas, Gary
The Sacred Marriage. Zondervan Publishing: 2002.

Jenkens, Jerry B.
Loving Your Marriage Enough To Protect It. Chicago: Moody, 1989, 1993.

Mylander, Charles; & Anderson, Neil T.
The Christ-Centered Marriage. California: Regal, 1996.

Paul, Robert S.,
Finding Ever After, Minneapolis: Bethany House, 2007.

Paul, Robert S., and Smalley, Greg
DNA of Relationships for Couples, Illinois: Tyndale House, 2006.

Rooks, Linda W.
Broken Heart on Hold: Surviving Separation. Cook Communication, Colorado Springs, 2006.

Shriver, Gary and Mona.
Unfaithful. Cook Communications, Colorado Springs, 2005.

Smalley, Gary; & Trent, John.
Love Is A Decision. Dallas: Word, 1989.

Smalley, Gary; Smalley, Greg; Paul, Robert S.,
DNA of Relationships, Illinois: Tyndale House, 2004.

Talley, Jim.
Reconcilable Differences. Nashville: Thomas Nelson, 1991.

Vernick, Leslie.
How To Act Right When Your Spouse Acts Wrong. Random House, 2001.

Warren, Neil Clark.
Make Anger Your Ally. Colorado: Focus on the Family, 1990.

Wright, Norman H.
Communication Key to Your Marriage. California: Regal, 1974.

WE WANT TO PRAY FOR YOU

We believe strongly in the power of prayer, and even though we may never personally meet you, we feel a connection with you because you are using our material. You can complete this page online at www.nationalmarriage.com, or remove this page and send it to the address below. Also feel free to help yourself to any of our other online support and resources.

May the Lord bless you.

Date: _____

Name:

First _____ Last _____

Address: _____

City: _____ State: _____ Zip: _____

Phone: (_____) _____

Marital Status: _____ Church Affiliation: _____

Is your spouse going through his/her own workbook also? Yes No

Do you have a support partner? Yes No

Are you attending a class? Yes No

Please use back of page to describe any additional prayer requests.

Thank You. Please remove this page and mail to:

National Institute of Marriage
2175 Sunset Inn Road
Branson, Missouri 65616

Thank you for providing your own envelope and postage.

www.ingramcontent.com/pod-product-compliance
Lightning Source LLC
Chambersburg PA
CBHW081500070526
44586CB00019B/2439